THE OUTDOOR ROOM

JAMIE DURIE
THE OUTDOOR ROOM

NEATH PORT TALBOT LIBRARIES

PHOTOGRAPHY BY SIMON KENNY

A SUE HINES BOOK
ALLEN & UNWIN

For architect Geoffrey Bawa, 1919–2003, who has been a constant source of inspiration to me.

First published in 2003

Copyright text © Jamie Durie 2003
Copyright photography © Simon Kenny 2003, except as indicated below

A Sue Hines Book
Allen & Unwin
83 Alexander Street
Crows Nest NSW 2065
Australia
Phone: (61 2) 8425 0100
Fax: (61 2) 9906 2218
Email: info@allenandunwin.com
Web: www.allenandunwin.com

National Library of Australia
Cataloguing-in-Publication entry:

Durie, Jamie.
The outdoor room.
ISBN 1 86508 788 2.
1. Gardens - Design. 2. Landscape gardening. 3. Landscape design. I. Kenny, Simon. II. Title.
712.6

The photographs on pages 13–18 are by Donna North and photographs on pages 112–13, 130, 132, 179 and endpapers by Harriet Rowe. All sketches and plans are by Patio.

The author and publishers are grateful to Anibou for their loan of the table used in the cover photograph and to the following companies for supplying images: alloy-homewares, House of Bamboo, Eco Concepts, Box & Dice, Fractal Systems (pp30–1); Eco Concepts, Urbanstone, Austimber Supplies, Rock 'n Stone, Fractal Systems (pp66–7); Made from Steel, Industree, House of Bamboo, Motyaj Potteries, Eco Concepts (pp88–9); Spence & Lyda, Bisque Interiors, Barlow Casual Furniture, alloy-homewares, Kezu (pp96–7); Clear Solutions Bathware (p135); Light on Landscapes (p199).

Designed and typeset by MAU Design
Printed in China through Colorcraft Ltd., Hong Kong

CONTENTS

INTRODUCTION WELCOME TO THE
OUTDOOR ROOM

Since the publication of *Patio*, I've been swamped with requests for more detailed information about how to achieve the distinctive look of the Patio designs featured in the book. Well, I could go on for several volumes about the technical side of things, but on the conceptual side, it's true to say that every one of my projects is based on simple principles and a combination of instinct and imagination. When the time came to sit down and write a second book, it made sense for me to concentrate on expanding those ideas and to share some of my theories and philosophies as well as a couple of trade secrets along the way.

Why the Outdoor Room? At the risk of sounding like a fanatic, I'm a firm believer that outdoor living spaces in our homes should be a whole lot more than just another place to carry out domestic activities. They have the potential to play a crucial role in nurturing personal wellbeing and in helping us to find both inner and outer peace in our daily lives. Exposure to fresh air, water, plants and sunshine immediately reconnects us to our essential humanity. When we live in the city – and most of us do – we can't climb a mountain, walk along a beach or wander through a forest every day, but we can endeavour to bring evocative symbols of these things into our homes.

No matter how large or small your exterior space, there's something in here for you. A big empty expanse is probably the hardest to start with because there are no boundaries, but step by step you can break it down into smaller, more intimate compartments for a series of fully livable locations. By the same token, don't think you need a minimum area to work with; even a small balcony can include all the basic elements of life. This then, is my definition of an outdoor room.

The following chapters cover what I believe to be the seven fundamental components of a beautiful and functional space. I haven't set out to write a technical manual – my aim is to provide inspiration balanced with a range of practical ideas and solutions. You'll see more detailed information here than in *Patio*, more hints and tips for you to apply. There are style guide pages, packed with products and materials that I use every day, and, of course, photographs speak for themselves so there's an abundance of gorgeous outdoor rooms to spark your imagination.

I've tried whenever I can to include suggestions to help you picture the results before you take the plunge. Using these visual aids is a good safety precaution but, more than that, it's a whole lot of fun to mess around building walls and stages out of boxes and broomsticks and sheets. Play is such an important part of the creative process, so forget about who's watching, just go for it and enjoy!

On a more sober note, in this era of global warming we can no longer ignore the devastating repercussions of human activity on this world of ours. The tremendous need for us all to work towards saving what's left of our beautiful planet is a major preoccupation of mine. You can see how this issue heavily influences my choice of plants, as most of them are hardy, robust and drought-resistant. You'll also see an emphasis on using sustainable organic materials like plantation timbers and bamboo and, wherever possible, choosing recycled or re-used commodities. Last but definitely not least, every chapter contains a special 'eco-tip' to help you make choices that will be less damaging to the environment and work towards ensuring a better future for our children.

I've loved making this book. The process of putting it together has forced me to reflect on some important life decisions and really clarify my design philosophy. It's also filled me with a new rush of enthusiasm for the enormous potential of our outdoor living spaces and the peace and pleasure they can bring us.

My hope is it will inspire you, too.

CHAPTER ONE THE
WALLS
DEFINING THE SPACE

Recently I was talking through ideas for this book with some friends, and was amazed at how many of them assumed that I always start with the floor when I begin a design. My reply was simply, 'You wouldn't put carpet down in an indoor room if there weren't any walls yet, so why would you lay a floor in an outdoor room if the area wasn't yet defined?' Whether walls are soft form (plant, screen) or hard form (stone, timber), they are ultimately what outlines the space so establishing where to position them and what kind of material they'll consist of can make or break the feel and the functionality of your outdoor room.

First and foremost, walls create intimacy and security. Remember what it felt like when you first spent the night in a tent? Only a thin slice of fabric between you and the elements but the sense of enclosure made you feel cosy and protected. The simple fact is that the larger the space the more it lacks the intimacy that characterises the outdoor room. A big country garden might be a daunting prospect to begin with, but you'd be amazed how you can instantly overcome this empty feeling by breaking it up into smaller compartments with solid or temporary partitions or by experimenting with levels.

Aesthetically, dressing the walls is a great opportunity to establish the personality of your outdoor room, providing a vertical canvas where you can express whatever you desire. Because of my theatrical background, I can't help thinking of this process as being like the process of dressing a stage: the screens are the wings, the levels are the platforms and the boundary walls are the rear curtains or backdrops. Then I work in the accent plants to act like props, the groundcovers to serve as smoke, dry ice or mist … you get the picture!

COR-TEN IS EASILY bent into unusual shapes, so it's the ideal material for this rambling, large-scale serpentine wall. Slicing through the landscape, the sheets overlap like fish scales and stand on their own strength and balance. The principle behind this structure was to create an organic sculptural form using hard geometrical steel with a natural weathered finish. It coils around the plant beds, contrasting starkly with soft, feathery drifts of grass. Horizontal sprays of water surge from between the cor-ten sheets, accentuating the dramatic movement of the curve. Behind the S-shaped curve is a blade wall made of sheets of cor-ten metal (overleaf), with rows of delicate silver-birch saplings embedded in a valley of soft black mulch between the blades. The surface of the cor-ten will rust over time, taking on the rich ochre hue seen here, but will not corrode to the point of decay.

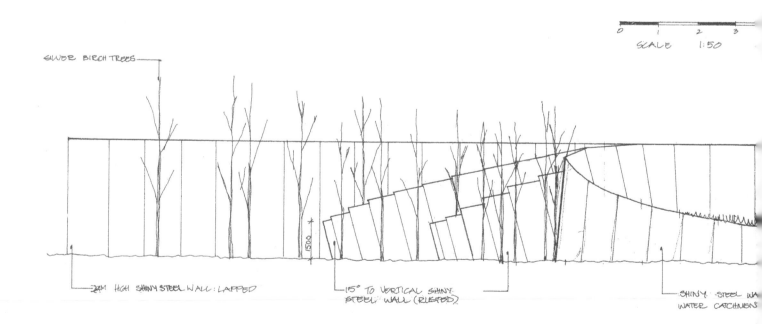

SHINY METAL WALL - 24t
RUSTED

SHINY METAL WALL
RUSTED - 24m t

BLUE METAL
LARGE FORMAT
(70-100mm).

SILVER
BIRCH

POND

SCALE   1:50

SILVER BIRCH TREES

24M HIGH SHINY STEEL WALL: LAPPED

15° TO VERTICAL SHINY
STEEL WALL (RUSTED)

SHINY STEEL WA
WATER CATCHMENS

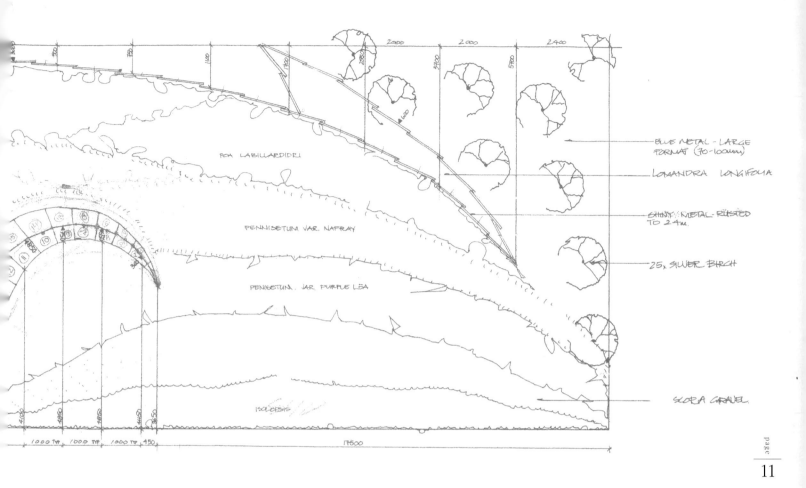

POA LABILLARDIDRI

PENNISETUM VAR. NAFRAY

PENNISETUM. VAR. PURPLE LEA

ISOLEPSIS

BLUE METAL - LARGE FORMAT (70-100mm)

LOMANDRA LONGIFOLIA

SHINY METAL - RUSTED TO 2.4m.

25x SILVER BIRCH

SCORIA GRAVEL.

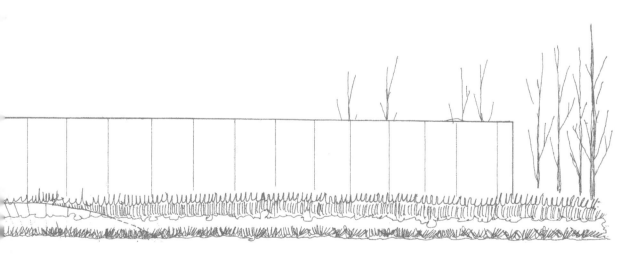

PLANT SCHEDULE

BOTANICAL NAME	COMMON NAME	SIZE	QTY.
Betula pendula	Silver Birch	3m	25
Isolepis nodosa	Knobby Club Rush	8"	
Lomandra longifolia	Spiny Headed Mat Rush	8"	
Pennisetum alopecuroides 'Nafray'	Swamp Foxtail Grass	8"	
Pennisetum alopecuroides 'Purple Lea'	Swamp Foxtail Grass	8"	
Phalaris arundinacea var. picta	Variegated Reedy Grass	8"	
Poa labillardiera	Poa	8"	

PROS AND CONS

Even before you start, make sure you're clear about how the room is going to be used. Will it be primarily a private refuge for contemplation and relaxation or will it need lots of seating options and open areas for entertaining the hordes? Then go out and have a good hard look at the space and identify what I call all the 'liabilities' and the 'assets'. For example, a liability could be a neighbour's window close to your property, a nearby highway or other intrusive traffic noise, a pedestrian path immediately outside or a backyard that overlooks yours. All these are potential trespassers infringing on your privacy, and they need to be screened or muffled as efficiently as possible.

One of your greatest assets could be an attractive view, however small. A bush or ocean outlook, a shady tree arching over a neighbour's fence, a glimpse of a city skyline – these fall under the category of assets. An indoor room that opens directly onto the outdoor room is also a huge advantage, especially if it's an entertainment area. Whatever you do, don't block access by placing things like planters between; keep the segue smooth with the lines flowing and you instantly blend two opposing spaces into one very versatile and interesting whole.

Now that you've decided where you want the walls to be, get out the old pencil and paper and draw some pictures. Don't hold back if you're not much of an artist: I'm a shocking scribbler myself but it's a great way of getting your ideas out of your head and onto paper so that you can start manipulating them into working dimensions. The next step might get you some strange looks but it's a brilliant way to test your ideas in situ. Grab a couple of broomsticks, string a rope between them and hang a sheet over the top to emulate where the potential wall would be. Leave it there for a day and you may discover a wall would block out vital sunlight at the most important time of the morning or afternoon. To be honest, this is also where you're going to have the most fun. Playing around with simple visual aids like this can get you really excited about what could be and shows you how to make the most of what's yours.

FINAL FRONTIER

Security is a must these days, especially in built-up areas. We've all got valuable possessions to protect, but most of all, we need to feel our families are safe from intruders. A solid wall is the decisive barrier for privacy and protection so, where budget permits, solid brick or stone is the strongest and most enduring option to go for. Otherwise, any wall over 1.8 metres tall constructed of a material that offers no possibility of a foothold can be considered secure.

THE THEME OF this garden, featured in the Ellerslie Flower Show in Auckland, New Zealand, is Australian landscape. A river divides the 'dry' side, representing the desert, and the 'wet' side, representing the rainforest. The spectacular cane sculptures rising from the water were directly inspired by the idea of Aboriginal fishing baskets, and the stepping-stones curled around them are reminiscent of swirling Aboriginal dot paintings.

THE ELLERSLIE SHOW is a wonderful opportunity for experimentation, and this one has some particularly innovative feature walls. Seen here are some super-sturdy barriers where panels of reinforcing mesh are attached to upright timber sleepers to form mini-cages. Filled with 50–150mm-diameter river pebbles, they can also be sectioned off horizontally to make windows. Every view was carefully planned for maximum effect.

DRIFTWOOD IS A marvellously evocative material to work with and here (top right) it forms a sculptural end-pillar to a plain rendered wall. Every piece was stacked to fit snuggly within the timber frame, bringing waves of movement and striking texture to a simple, functional boundary.

If you want to disguise the base material, there's a wide selection of finishes available, from tile-cladding to a range of different renders. Bagging is probably one of the easiest finishes to apply. A thin coating of sand and cement mix is sponged on to give a uniform texture while still showing the uneven surface of the bricks or stones beneath. At the other end of the spectrum you have methods like Spanish rendering where a coating of the mix is pasted on in thick random smears, much like spreading a layer of peanut butter on toast. As for the colour finish, there's an enormous palette to choose from so it's up to you whether to highlight it as a feature wall or encourage it to blend in with the surroundings.

Timber is a fantastic permanent wall and can be as sturdy as stone, depending on the way it's constructed. A simple treated-pine timber paling fence is structurally sound, won't rot, and laid butt-to-butt will prevent an intruder from gaining a foot- or hand-hold. Ensure you have a decent-sized cap (at least 45mm x 120mm) at the top and the bottom and you have all the strength you need as well as a nice sturdy look. Best of all, you are using a renewable resource and that's got to be good.

If you need strength, but wish to avoid the 'blockiness' of a solid wall, timber palings can be swivelled on edge to make a vertical shutter. Timbers are placed so they angle

TIMBER SCREENS

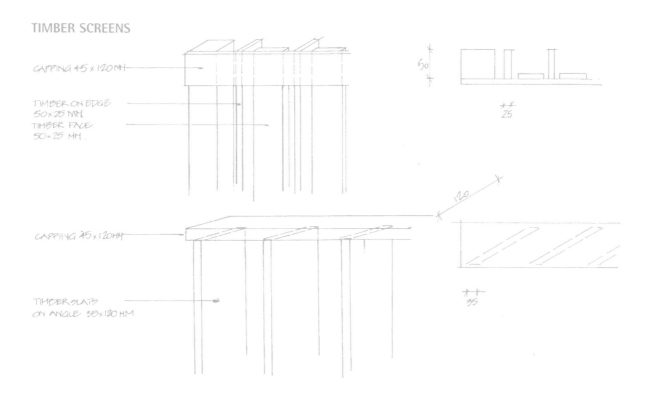

THE STANDARD TIMBER paling fence need not be visually dull, as we see here, with every second plank laid on edge (above) and with the timbers fixed on an angle assuring privacy and the continued flow of light and air (below).

towards your biggest liability, screening it from view. Spaced with roughly 75mm between, a series of 25 x 110mm boards will give you plenty of ventilation with enough light to keep the backs of shrubs thriving and less risk of fungal disease on your plants.

Alternatively, you can sink treated pine sleepers about 700mm into the ground in a soldier-course formation (neatly parallel and evenly spaced). Firmly encased in a concrete footing they are an inpenetrable boundary and will need no other form of support. Try experimenting with paint – a different colour for every face – which accentuates the form of the timber. Set some low-voltage lights between the sleepers for a dramatic night-time effect where slim shafts of light shoot off into the darkness.

I love the look of a rippling S-shaped serpentine wall. Its gentle, sinuous curves create niches that present a perfect opportunity to show off interesting plants or features. Best of all, it provides its own structural support requiring only basic footings because each opposing radius offsets the other.

Semi-spaced block-work walls are making a welcome comeback. This is where you construct a lattice-like boundary by leaving gaps between the bricks. The method has long been popular with commercial properties, but it can look fabulous in a domestic environment where the openings created by the missed bricks become ready-made shelves for pots or pieces of art. You can have lots of fun with paint, too. Try one colour on the face and a contrast on the sides so that as you move alongside it a two-tone effect springs out at the viewer. Like the serpentine wall, this one is also very flexible and can turn easily because the bricks are not positioned butt-to-butt.

THE SOMETIMES SCREEN

Semi-permanent partitions and screens are what I call 'temporary' divisions which can provide shade, a gentle border, a sense of privacy and the delightful bonus of atmospheric elements like shadows and dappled light. I tend to favour natural materials for the way they drift in the breeze and diffuse the sunlight.

TIMBER SCREEN

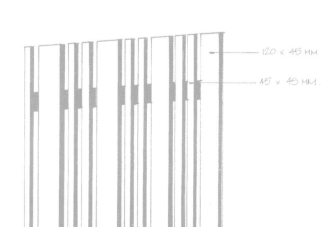

120 x 45 MM

45 x 45 MM

SOLDIER–COURSE SLEEPER SCREEN

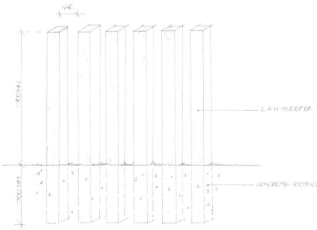

VAR.

2.4 M SLEEPER

CONCRETE FOOTING

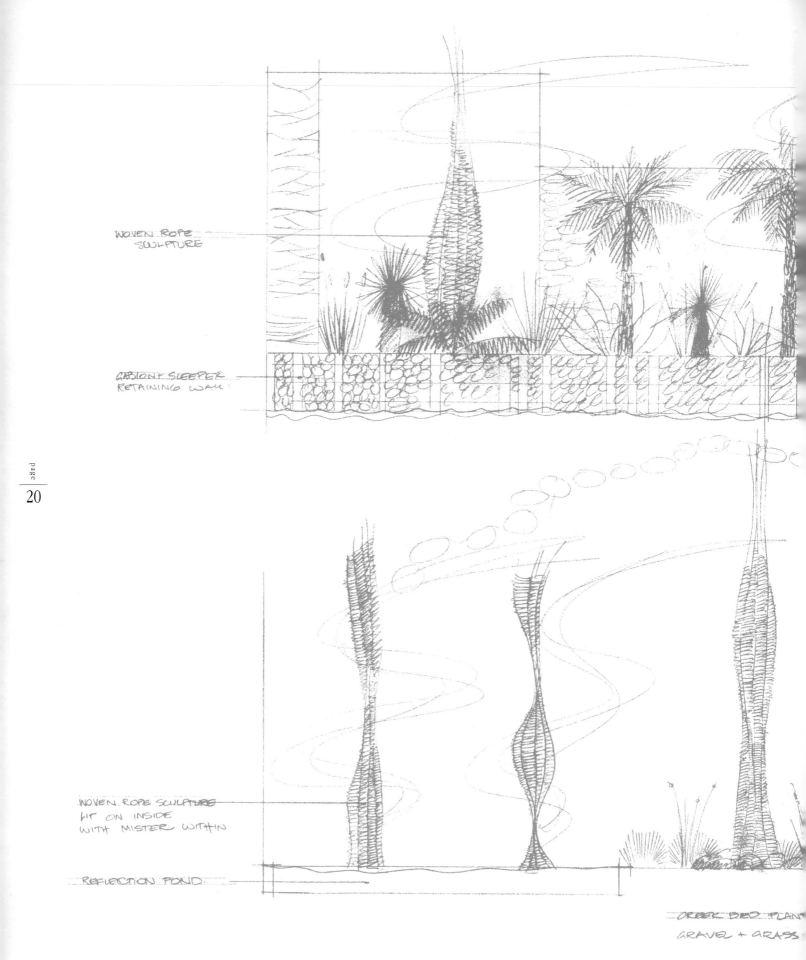

WOVEN ROPE
SCULPTURE

GABION + SLEEPER
RETAINING WALL

WOVEN ROPE SCULPTURE
LIT ON INSIDE
WITH MISTER WITHIN

REFLECTION POND

CREEK BED PLANT

GRAVEL + GRASS

SECTION.

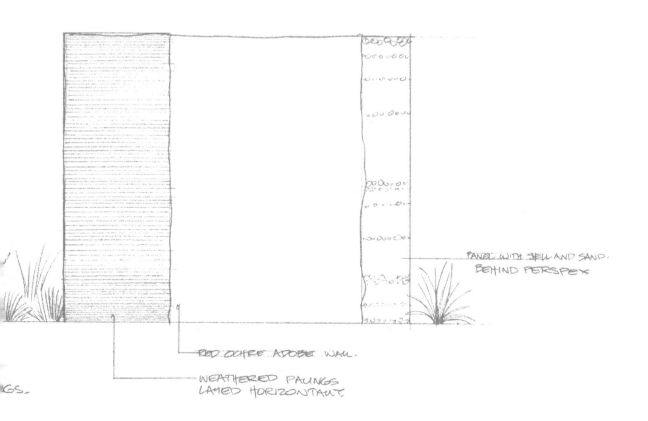

PANEL WITH SHELL AND SAND.
BEHIND PERSPEX

RED OCHRE ADOBE WALL.

WEATHERED PALINGS
LAYED HORIZONTALLY.

Reed blinds (again, I recommend Natureed) make a fine linear partition, and the reeds making up the sheets come in a variety of width measurements from anywhere between 5mm and 75mm. Bamboo screens are excellent light filters and I'm particularly fond of the Japanese versions which are lashed together with rope rather than nailed together so they are entirely organic.

Sails continue to be a popular screen choice, but canvas is rarely used these days as it's had to make way for the more durable plastic. Traditionally used for shading, sails are a wonderful vertical partition and allow you to play with vibrant colours and different shapes. Don't limit yourself with the kinds of materials you choose for screening. As long as a product can withstand the elements, you can use it anywhere in the space, so think outside the square.

GREEN WALL

Fresh, tactile and fabulous to look at, nothing beats a layered bank of shrubs and perennials, curtains of delicate climbers and perhaps a tree or two towering at the back. I see the transition from groundcover to shrub to tree as part of a single plant zone, so my green wall might constitute an area that extends back as far as two or three metres. But before you dive in and begin planting, make sure the conditions are right. Is there enough sun to encourage a decent spread of tree foliage, for example? Is the soil deep enough, rich enough and well

SURROUNDED BY LESS *dominant plants, this* Echium *(Pride of Madeira, left) is a lush centrepiece to a textural green wall. In summer the mounds of grey-green foliage form a cloudy backdrop to the resplendent spires of its brilliant blue flowers.* MASSIVE TERRAZZO PLANTERS *outside this busy city shopping complex (centre) hold a self-contained green screen with large drooping fronds of* Strelitzia nicolai *and Fan Palms.* A MAGNIFICENT STAND *of Stripy Bamboo (*Bambusa multiplex *cv., right), its sturdy, tapering trunks softened by wispy clusters of leaves.*

enough drained to support a variety of root formations? Is the soil sandy or does it have a heavy clay content?

Then comes the choice of plants, and this is where knowledge is the key. Only when you know the potentials and limitations of a variety of species do you have the tools to sculpt your wall successfully. I would recommend you systematically go through the plants available, and the best way to do this is to get your hands on a Botanica. (I never leave home without one!) A good quality plant reference manual will tell you all the basics about what the plant needs to survive and how big it will grow and usually it will provide a picture alongside the plant description so you can visualise how it will look in the space. Once you've studied the plants' survival characteristics, choose those that are appropriate to the shape, colour and texture you desire and the specific conditions of your space.

Another good idea is to go for a walk around your local Botanic Gardens taking note of the magnificent varieties of plants available and checking the labels as you go. When I was studying horticulture I would steal away whenever possible and eat my lunch walking around the Botanic Gardens. I learnt a huge amount from these brief wanders and, I must admit, not a day goes by when I don't miss those peaceful and inspirational lessons.

Keep in mind that different plants develop in different ways so you need to identify which types of growth will suit the purposes of your outdoor room.

HEDGING is the obvious green wall and thankfully, we've come a long way from the generic Box hedge. Lilly pilly makes a wonderful thick boundary, as do *Pittosporum* 'James Stirling', camellias, photinias, murrayas, viburnums and robinias. Some eucalypts work well for a lighter structure, along with *Michelia figo*, NZ flax, *Westringia* spp. and even coprosmas for a beachfront property. Any of the clumping bamboos do a fine job of providing vertical cover while still allowing light to filter through.

ALL THE BEST ideas are right in front of you, and more often than not, they come from nature – note the incredible formation of these branches. This Dracaena draco *lives in Sydney's Botanic Gardens. As you can see, we're very close.*

AERIAL PLEACHING is the method whereby you strip back all the lower branches of the shrub to reveal the trunk and the outstretched branches above join up to form a continuous canopy. Lilly pillies, pittosporums, robinias, pears and citrus work particularly well, but make sure the plants are not so close that they crowd together and bulge. What you're aiming for is a continuous wall of green where the tips of the laterally spreading upper foliage touch to create a solid aerial hedge. A finely pleached hedge looks magnificent up-lit against a wall or if free-standing it can form an arched window channelling the eye towards a garden view beyond. Pleaching also encourages the growth of a lower storey of foliage because the light coming through the naked trunks ensures a level of contrasting shrubbery can thrive below.

CLIMBERS are great for disguising an ugly surface. Twining and scrambling plants work around what's there whereas root climbers make their mark on the surroundings. *Ficus pumila* is one of the most aggressive and adhesive climbers I know with shoots that will eventually work their way into the brickwork. If you trim off the adolescent trunk and woody build-up and keep it all immature growth, the *Ficus* will maintain a tight, compact cover. Keep an eye on this one because it can get away from you and it's hard to get rid of once it's established, but this truly is the ultimate growing wall that will retain its architecture forever.

A SCREEN WALL can be used to draw people in to a garden or to frame a view. Fencing an area will also encourage the viewer to focus on a part of the garden they might not have noticed (left). PAVING COVERS MOST of this substantial suburban outdoor room (right) so treated pine fencing was deliberately chosen to contrast with its hard angular lines. The horizontal timber baton screens are fixed in an alternating double layer so neighbours can't see in, but the void in between allows light and breezes to pass through. A pillar water feature breaks up the lengthy wooden expanse.

the simple things

Garden design is constantly evolving – that's just one of the reasons why I'm hooked. I'm still relatively new to this career, and although I've learnt a great deal in five years, I'm well aware there's so much more to know. You never stop coming across new techniques, absorbing new ideas and, little by little, gaining the confidence to trust your instincts. I'm forever being surprised and challenged by the possibilities presented to me and delighted by the reactions of my clients when the picture in my head translates into a reality before their eyes.

Several months back I designed a series of outdoor rooms for a young businessman and his partner. The property was stunning: lavish and opulent with some breathtaking features. They loved what we did to the place, but funnily enough, their favourite addition ended up being a small, simple outdoor yoga room with clean lines and minimal fittings.

A classic example of that wise and wonderful adage: Less Is More.

Other less aggressive climbers on my list of favourites are Chilean Jasmine (*Mandevilla*), Madagascar Jasmine (*Stephanotis* sp.) and *Hardenbergia* with its pretty purple flower. If you want to cover up an old wall in a hurry, put in a passionfruit vine which will spread swiftly and be laden with fruit in the summer months.

ESPALIER is a rare sight these days, but to me there's nothing more elegant than a fruiting or flowering wall smothered in fragrant blossoms. It's a time-consuming process which involves a fair bit of finicky work whereby all the front and rear branches are pruned back and the lateral branches are trained along a trellis, cable or fence. However, if you do decide to commit time and energy to an espaliered wall, the rewards are great, especially if you choose a shrub that both flowers and fruits, allowing you to observe the seasons changing and enjoy its bounty all year round. Camellias, roses and star jasmine are good options.

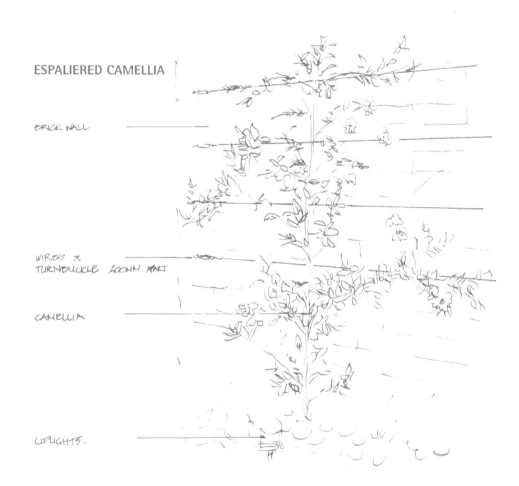

ESPALIERED CAMELLIA

BRICK WALL

WIRES x
TURNBUCKLE 200MM APART

CAMELLIA

UPLIGHTS.

inspiration
WALLS

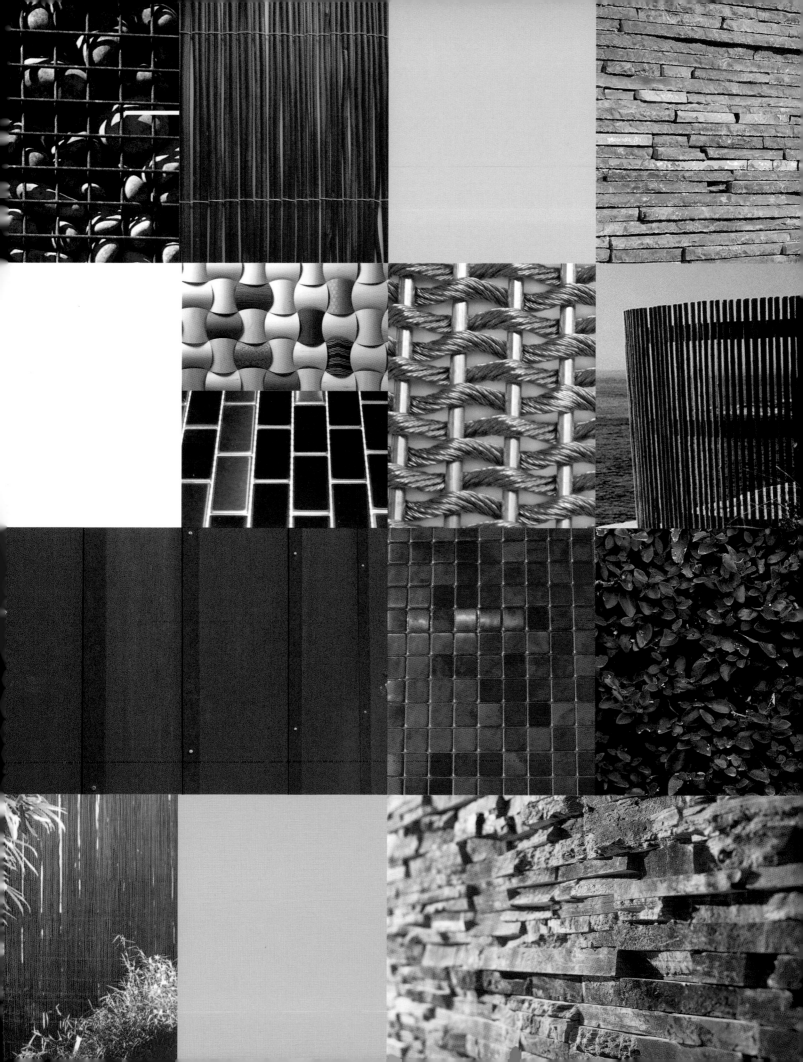

above and beyond

Complete or partial ceilings aren't a priority in most outdoor rooms, but there are few that wouldn't benefit from a degree of overhead cover. I've had clients who like to do as much living outside as possible – rain, hail or shine – so they need constant protection from the changing elements. You might have a piece of furniture or artwork or some sound equipment that isn't weatherproof. You might have a particularly exposed space and want to incorporate some kind of permanent shield from the harmful effects of the harsh antipodean sun. Then there are the statistics that tell us more and more Australians are choosing to work from home. I can't imagine a more pleasant and energising space to locate part or all of your home office than your outdoor room (but you might need additional shelter to protect computer hardware and so on).

Corrugated plastic products are an extremely cost-effective option. As long as the sheets are fixed on at least a 5-degree angle, water won't build up and stagnate between the layers. Glass and perspex form a clean, clear protective shield, and I recommend some timber slats over the top to provide shade.

PRIME TIME FOR *showing off the alang-alang pavilion is evening. Strategically placed globes project a mellow, honeyed wash, highlighting the tightly wound batons of* Imperata *grass to perfection. Restful and airy by day, the room takes on an extraordinary feeling of warmth and intimacy when plunged into darkness.*

Sailcloths are a great cover but be aware that they are not all waterproof and sunproof. Materials range from 20 per cent UV protection to total blockout so choose the right product for the right situation.

Personally, I like to feel that I'm surrounded with as much organic material as possible so most of my favourite shade structures are made of natural products that allow light and air to filter through. You can disguise the more austere structures by cladding with timber, bamboo, Natureed or branches of tea-tree.

My all-time number one roof structure would have to be the thatched 'alang-alang' pergola from Indonesia. Impervious to moisture, its waterproofing capacity increases with the years because the principal material, the grass *Imperata cylindrica*, packs down and knits together in much the same way as feathers on a duck's back. The interior detail of the alang-alang is stunning. I love gazing up at the neat wads of grass wrapped tightly around bamboo rods in perfect symmetry. And the fragrance of the thatching material is spicy and evocative, instantly transporting me back to my beloved Bali.

HERE WE SEE *how the alang-alang roof was deliberately tilted towards the viewer to emphasise its intricate internal structure. Lush plantings, incremental level changes, a shallow pool embracing the forecourt and a rich purple retaining wall along the back all contribute to a sense of peaceful sanctuary.*

THAI SILK BOLSTERS *(below) supply*
flamboyant colour to contrast with tawny timber
and golden thatch, while the detail of the alang-
alang ceiling (below right) is surely a work of art
in itself.

CHAPTER TWO THE
FLOOR
A BASE ON WHICH TO BUILD

Now that you've shaped your space, it's time for the groundwork to begin. The floor – and by that I mean everything that sits on the ground of the outdoor room – is an intrinsic part of its visual impact, connecting and unifying all the different elements, blending inside and out and being touched in some way by every single person who enters.

Steps, decks or platforms and pathways are a vital structural consideration and must be built around the same time as fixing the walls. However, the material for the floor will often be the last thing you decide on because it will be dictated by things like the prevailing colour theme, the choice of plants, the placement of tables and chairs and the amount of wear and tear it will have to cope with.

The good news is that the technology of floor products has advanced in leaps and bounds. Pavers installed at Homebush for the 2000 Sydney Olympics were a world-famous example of this. A series of modular interlocking pieces riddled with tiny holes that allowed water to run through just like natural soil, they reduce the run-off that pollutes our drainage system and precious oceans. Exciting innovations like these are just the tip of the iceberg when it comes to exterior floor surfaces.

I use stone and pavers a lot because they are so practical for high traffic areas, but wherever appropriate I will install a surface that encourages people to decrease the pace a little. This comes from a Japanese philosophy, to slow down the viewer so they appreciate what's around them more. A good way of achieving this is to build large wooden pontoons in stepping-stone formation (or just put in some stepping stones) and then plant everything in between and around them. Not only do you feel light and elevated (almost a floating sensation), but because the path is broken up, you're gently coerced into taking that little bit of extra care with your steps and consequently a little more time to soak up the surroundings. Obviously, if you've got to wheel your bin or bicycle through there, you'll need to join up the pontoons for easier access, but this is still a fine technique for enhancing the enjoyment of the outdoor room.

LEVEL-HEADED

Once in a blue moon I'll find myself in a big space with a client staring at me in eager anticipation and I'm completely stuck for ideas. Then suddenly I'll picture a series of raised flowerbeds or a sunken dining area and the creative juices instantly start flowing again.

Introducing a change of level, even as small as 250mm, can transform a space, and the evidence of this is all around us. Nature knows no bounds when it comes to levels: trees and shrubs are random heights and ever-changing; mountains, valleys, cliffs and ravines are all part of a structural template that we can pick up on and bring into our gardens. It may not be so easy to achieve inside our homes, but the outdoors lend themselves to such creativity.

Start with the section where you're going to spend the most time, whether relaxing or entertaining, and work on achieving a 'sunken' feel so that it's more enclosed and intimate.

If there's a section with an outlook, think about raising it to capitalise on the view. (A sunbathing area that looks down on the pool is a fine opportunity to do this.)

DESIGNED AS A busy public thoroughfare, the abundance of this space presented a fabulous opportunity to introduce natural elements into what is traditionally a very corporate environment. Slashing through an ordered promenade of paving is a narrow creek bed fringed with river stones and reeds. Just a glimpse of this trickling waterway makes you want to take off your shoes and socks and go for a refreshing paddle.

MINIATURE STARBURSTS *of* Pieris 'Red Mill' *sweep the earth beneath Chinese Elms* (Ulmus parvifolia), *alleviating the hefty bulk of the basalt blocks that make up the retaining wall.*

'JUST LIKE THE COMBINATION OF SOMETHING OLD AND SOMETHING NEW, THE MARRIAGE OF NATURAL FORM AND MAN-MADE INTRODUCES A LOVELY SENSE OF BALANCE.'

A VERITABLE CATALOGUE *of floor options. Through the sentry-like timber screen painted to complement the autumn colours (left), mounds of deep crimson* Loropetalum *'Burgundy' lead to an* Acer palmatum *'Globosum' (Plane Tree) on a bed of* Pieris *'Red Mill' interspersed with chalky white pebbles for contrast. Stepping-stones traverse the slow-moving creek bed (right), banked by river stones and reeds and clumps of* Isolepsis nodosa *(Knobby Club Rush) and* Lomandra hystrix *(Matt Rush).*

Elevating plant beds makes caring for your plants easier and highlights the structure and form of the leaves, but do ensure that drainage is adequate to cope with the run-off. And, of course, when you're planning stairs and levels, keep in mind wheelchair and pram access as well as the needs of any elderly friends and family.

Visualising changing levels in the mind's eye is a skill that I hope will never leave me, but for many people, this is not something that comes easily. Fortunately, anyone can trial the look they're going for by building temporary stages out of planks, milk crates, cardboard boxes and anything else that will demonstrate how a change of level will affect the room. It might look a bit like a *Play School* set, but it really works.

Small courtyards rarely need them, but clearly defined pathways are a must in a large garden, guiding the feet and leading the eye to features and destinations. Unless it's a primarily functional space, I prefer a curved, meandering path. Even the more formal, linear gardens benefit from a bending pathway which introduces a subtle visual balance.

A word of warning: don't fall into the trap of getting so carried away that the trail ends up too complex. People will become bored winding back and forth with no apparent reason, so make sure there's a purpose to every twist and turn.

STICKS AND STONES

Probably the biggest decision you'll have to make about the floor is the type of material you'll choose. Much will depend on how the room will be used. Will it have to put up with kids' wear and tear? Will your pets spend a lot of time out there? Or will it be primarily ornamental so the look and feel of it is the top priority? Bear in mind that light colours open up a smaller space, making it look larger. And a hot space in full sun for much of the day will benefit from a lightly tinted floor surface that won't reflect the light or promote a feeling of stuffiness.

PAVERS fit the bill in just about any situation. They're hardy, versatile, cost-effective and come in every colour of the rainbow. Laying them is relatively easy:

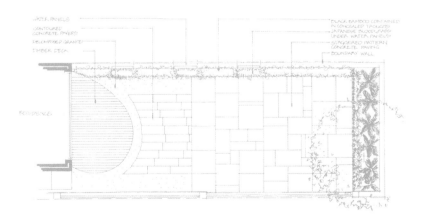

ONE LEVEL MADE up of four distinctly different floor materials makes this small courtyard look much larger and provides plenty of visual interest.

either on a concrete base for vehicular weights or a more pliable road base mixture for your average daily human traffic. The only other questions you need to concern yourself with are the number of grout lines you want and which direction the pattern should run across the space.

TURF is a traditional favourite but it needs a steady supply of water, regular fertilizing and pesticide to keep it looking good all year round. I tell my clients, if you have kids then it's probably worth it, but otherwise I would always prefer to see a space filled with a rich spread of plant life interrupted by paths and niches,

platforms and decks. It's simple really: you're creating a garden because there's something about nature that you like, but a lawn all but defeats that purpose by flattening the original landscape and covering it over.

STONE comes in a multitude of fantastic textural finishes such as honed (an unpolished matt surface with a sheen), bush-hammered (an even surface studded with pocks for grip and texture) and split-face (a roughly chipped, highly uneven surface). Then there are all the wonderful reconstructed stone like terrazzo where crushed aggregates are bonded together in concrete and polished back to give a great retro look.

Pebbles have become hugely popular in the garden, but to be honest, I question where some of them come from. I was a big fan until I started doing research on where they originate and was horrified to discover that many tons are lifted off beaches and pulled out of riverbeds in countries where water is in short supply. You see, pebbles are one of nature's filtering systems, and if they are removed from an already struggling waterway, the liquid that remains quickly becomes rank and contaminated. So if you're covering a large area, please think about using them conservatively by mixing them in with other surface materials (like recycled concrete, for example) and avoiding the piled-up look. Lately, I've started encouraging people to use crushed stone rather than pebbles. Quartz, granite, sandstone or recycled crushed concrete are just some of the great-looking alternatives available.

CREAMY CLAY TILES look fantastic against pale greys and delicate blues – colours that remind us of a crystal ocean and pristine sandy beach (left). EXTERIOR TIMBER FLOORS (centre) weather and age with the changing seasons, and can provide a strong visual link between indoors and out. PONTOONS SLOW DOWN the viewer, encouraging us to take a bit more time observing the surroundings. This gently undulating pontoon pathway (right) picks its way through a carpet of groundcovers, spot-planted shrubs and sunken sleepers.

THE OWNERS OF *this comfortable Federation home wanted to get rid of the struggling lawn which took up most of their outdoor area, so the small paved section of split-face sandstone which had aged to a lovely soft grey was extended to become the dominant ground surface. As you can see on the following pages, when the sandstone is new it's a much paler beige, but with time and weather it will end up blending with the old section. Garden beds were built up in keeping with the existing green-scape which has a distinct tropical flavour. The result is a leafy array of lush shade- and moisture-loving species.*

USING A VARIED SELECTION of rocks and pebbles, this sculpted floor surface inevitably becomes a feature in itself.

Cool and elegant, stone brings an aura of luxury and opulence to any room, but you need to carefully pick the areas where you use it. Honed stone is dangerous as a pool surround because of its slippery finish, and a delicate glass dropped on stone will shatter into a million tiny shards that could haunt your entertainment area for months. Food and drink on an unsealed surface can lead to stains, with red wine a major culprit. A careless splash of shiraz will leave an everlasting pink reminder.

CONCRETE is a versatile, inexpensive contemporary surface, and when finished in the right way it can look very impressive. There are lots of ways you can alter the texture and it takes colour brilliantly, but make sure the pigment or oxide is mixed directly into the concrete rather than painted on top as surface paint wears quickly,

especially in busy areas. One of my favourite finishes is exposed aggrogate, where the concrete is sprayed with a high-pressure hose before it has fully cured, washing away the top layer and exposing the flecks of stone or aggregate in the mix.

CERAMIC tiles can be a stunning focal point, but I usually use them in covered spaces because once water gets onto a tile you're skating on ice. The same goes for glass and resin. Generally installed in sheets or tile form, they are an expensive option so better to use them as a highlight material (especially in conjunction with light and water) rather than the main event.

WOOD is one of the most neutral, controllable materials you can get your hands on. Cool in summer and warm in winter, it's deliciously tactile and is one of the only surfaces you can picture yourself lying on

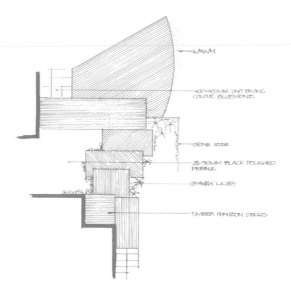

LAWN

400×400MM UNIT PAVING
COLOUR BLUESTONE.

STONE EDGE

25-50MM BLACK POLISHED
PEBBLE.

CANNA LILIES

TIMBER PONTOON DECKS

A SERIES OF *differently shaped overlapping decks*
descend through this outdoor room, with the
timbers laid in various directions to guide the eye
towards special points of interest in the garden.

wearing a pair of swimmers without a towel in
between. There are thousands of neglected
timber decks out there giving wood a bad
name, but minimal maintenance is all it
requires to serve you well for many years. It's
a myth that wood doesn't cope well in the
elements – trees come from outside, after all.
Once the timber is cut it continues to breathe,
expanding and contracting with the seasons,
so you simply allow for that by nurturing it
like any other living organism. Think of it as
just another growing element to the garden
that requires feeding and maintenance, and
like a well-kept plant, it will pay you back
many times with its soft healthy glow, silky
smoothness underfoot, and strength and
durability.

Treated pine is a plantation timber that
responds beautifully to stains and oiling.
(A quick tip is to buy boiled oil which is
free of the organisms that cause mould and
mildew patches.) There are different ratings of
treatment to be aware of before you buy: H5
means it can be immersed in fresh water, H4
means it can be sunk in ground. All treated
timbers are vermin-proof and will resist mould
and rot. Remember that once you cut it, you
must re-treat the exposed portion with a
preserva-tive like copper napthinate, because
even the smallest untreated area opens the way
for potentially damaging organisms to spoil
the whole piece.

And finally, when decking planks are
assembled, ensure they have at least 3mm gap
between them. A timber deck will buckle,
warp or split only when the boards are banked
up too tightly against each other, much like a
wisdom tooth grows through the gum and
forces the other teeth forward.

favourite growing floors

Well, I've told you already how I feel about lawn, but there are some fantastic low-maintenance groundcovers that really shine in small spaces or as complementary borders for bricks and pavers.

Ajuga reptans 'Atropurpurea' (Bugle Weed) has a dark, lush, burgundy foliage.

Pratia pedunculata (Matted Pratia) is flat and fine-leafed with tiny white or blue flowers.

Ophiopogon japonicus (Mondo Grass) forms soft, spiky dark-green clumps.

Heterocentron elegans (Spanish Shawl) has a vivid pink flower and fine green leaves making it an attractive two-toned cover.

Sagina subulata (Pearlwort) is spongy and robust with a fine-leafed surface.

Dichondra repens (Kidney Weed) forms a clover-like carpet.

Soleirolia soleirolii (Baby's Tears) is delicate and mossy and grows well in shade.

Grevillea 'Poorinda Royal Mantle' (Royal Mantle Grevillea) is a thick, rambling groundcover which is great for stabilising banks.

Hardenbergia violacea (False Sarsparilla) has a long dark-green leaf and a delicate purple flower.

Viola hederacea (Native Violet) is soft and clover-like with tiny purple and white blooms.

LEFT TO RIGHT: Dianella *sp.*, Carpobrotus edulis, Loropetalum *'Burgundy'*, Ajuga reptans.

THERE'S A SUPERB atmosphere of cosiness and
wellbeing in this courtyard, and the floor surfaces
have a lot to do with the success of the overall
effect. Slabs of sandstone cut into random
geometric shapes are laid in simple, ornamental
form, bringing a light, reflective quality to the
shady space. Smooth decking breaks the sandstone
into mini arenas, banding the garden beds and
echoing the solid bench seat which faces a small
fountain trickling from the hollowed centre
of a block of lava stone. With sturdy rendered
brick walls, there's a pervading sense of privacy and
security so the owners can relax completely and
enjoy the full benefits of their outdoor room.

THE LARGE-FORMAT floor slabs resonate with the chunky blocks of this low retaining wall. The key here is the strip of timber that divides vertical and horizontal sandstone, emphasising the marriage of identical materials but very different textures.

SLEEK AND SMOOTH to the touch, this stretch of timber platform (below left) glows warmly under low-voltage lighting. A variety of timber widths introduce a subtle decorative element, proving once again that with a little imagination there is tremendous visual potential in a simple wooden surface. Well-concealed lighting illuminates the pond (below right), a radiant miniature stage draped in a forest of gilded leaves and stems.

THIS VIEW ENCOMPASSES *much of what I love about the outdoor room. With the doors folded back, inside and out dissolve into a single, wholly livable space. Carpet becomes wood becomes sandstone becomes plant. The plain timber desk and chair match the timber bench, and puddles of directional light bathe the chosen points of interest, uniting all facets of the interior and exterior. Note the storage space that complements rather than intrudes. The lofty timber cupboard pictured behind the glass door holds all the bulky garden equipment and conceals the obligatory water meter.*

FLOORS
inspiration

CHAPTER THREE THE
FURNISHINGS
HOLD THE BODY, PLEASE THE EYE

This is where creativity really kicks in. With all the structural elements in place, the next step is to introduce the magnets that will entice a body to sit or recline or dine, the containers that will present swatches of living colour and texture, and all the extras that will make the outdoor room as comfortable and convenient as the rooms inside.

For many, presentation is the main focus. As a visual person I can thoroughly relate to this, but I would never sacrifice functionality for aesthetics, especially when it comes to a much-used living area. The trick, as always, is to find the right balance, and I have a simple theory with which I've had overwhelming success: the more you can design in situ that's permanent (like built-in benches), the better the space will look all year round. It's just like having a permanently made-up bed. Alternatively, design your commodities and

equipment so they can be easily folded up or tucked away. More and more of my clients are asking for tables that can be swung up and stored flush with the wall, freeing up valuable space. And custom-made furnishing always looks that little bit more attractive because it's unique to the location.

There's a lot to be said for gardens that only require minimal maintenance, and for people with busy lives it may be a necessity, but I think owners who eliminate the need for any upkeep whatsoever are missing out. Even the simplest task is a creative act: from tending a small tub of flowers to oiling a wooden deckchair. When you actively care for your garden it becomes more valuable and you don't take it for granted. Even the smallest chore means you've invested in the space – it's become part of your life – so I love to see owners interacting with their garden.

PLACING PEOPLE

Positioning the various pieces in your outdoor room is as straightforward as furnishing your loungeroom. Identify the main feature (water, accent plants or sculpture draws the eye just like a television), and arrange your seats and lounges at the best vantage points. Then make your adjustments according to where the sun falls throughout the day, perhaps rigging up a bamboo blind to shield a swing chair from afternoon glare or shifting the breakfast table so it's bathed in morning light. Similarly, don't put the main point of congregation in an exposed area: nothing is worse than being blown about or being cooked in the midday sun while you're trying to eat a meal or read the paper.

Take note of the outlook from each position and ensure that no-one winds up staring at a blank wall. And instead of forcing everyone in the dining area to sit at the table all the time, try to arrange it so that one end snuggles up against some informal bench seating so people can move there for more intimate conversation before and after eating. Even better, corner niches are a great chat zone, and you should fully exploit all the corners or right angles in your seating formation so that people can interact face-to-face.

I make no apology for being a rabid promoter of bench seating – it is without doubt a signature part of my outdoor rooms. A free-standing armchair eats up lots of precious space, whereas benches are part of the perimeter itself. Benches are the best way to keep the space looking clean and uncluttered. They are sleek and immovable so you can maintain your original style forever which is a great way of policing the design integrity and ensuring that it remains true.

ALTHOUGH THIS BENCH is lowered by what looks to be a negligible amount, it's a significant level change that entices the viewer to sit or recline. Hinged at one end, it tilts into an adjustable back-rest which can be softened with cushions and bollards stored within the bench void. Yuccas (Yucca elephantipes) *are uplit to make the most of their starburst foliage, and the spot-planted Baby's Tears* (Soleirolia soleirolii) *will quickly spread and join up to form a mossy groundcover.*

BENCH SEATING

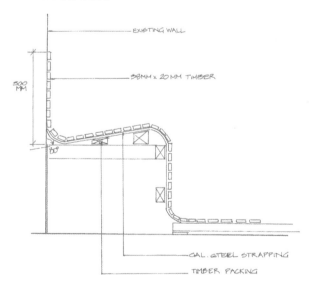

EXISTING WALL

38MM x 20MM TIMBER

500 MM

60

GAL. STEEL STRAPPING

TIMBER PACKING

AT NIGHT YOU can really see how levels play a major part in every aspect of this outdoor room. The effect is intimate yet spacious, and the furnishings are discreet and versatile.

THE DELICIOUS MAGNOLIA (left) and frangipani flowers (right) smell almost good enough to eat. I love their creamy petals, and the rosy spectrum of colour within the frangipani reminds me of a tropical sunset.

A bench is far nicer to look at than a retaining wall, and it introduces a new level that softens the hard vertical angle of the sheer face. Best of all it's a great magnet, a place of rest that gives people a reason to go out there and appreciate what the room and garden beyond have to offer.

Lumbar support is a bit of a preoccupation of mine, not only because I'm concerned about back health, but also to encourage people to feel they can sprawl out. In custom-made benches I'll insert a small timber support-dome in the slats about 220mm up from the base of the bench. Cushions are optional but can bring a lovely tactile element. Their colours also help theme the room, and a vividly exotic Thai fabric or striking tribal print might become the decisive unifying element. Marine canvas is one of the hardiest fabrics, but you can experiment by waterproofing other fabrics. Log cushions are a good alternative where a bench design doesn't include built-in lumbar support.

Though it will cost more to build, hinging your benches so that the tops flip up revealing voids for useful storage is a brilliant way to maintain the original look of the space. And you can tuck cushions out of sight whenever they're not in use, ensuring the cushion fabric will have a longer life.

If you don't want to go all the way and use built-in benches, think about the width of the capping on your retaining walls. Design them no lower than 420mm or higher than 550mm and between 450mm and 600mm wide and you have a handy surface for seating, display and numerous other purposes.

SUNKEN SEATING

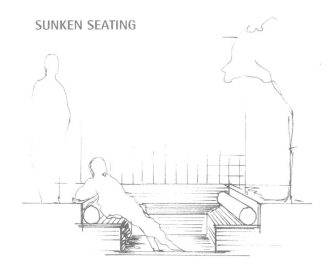

STRONG, CLEAN LINES, *simple planting and a sense of space and elongation was the brief for this narrow courtyard. To divert attention from the overlooking apartments, a water feature extends along the boundary. The liquid trickles from emitters at the top and slides across slender resin shelves which look particularly attractive lit up at night, taking on a faintly luminous quality.*

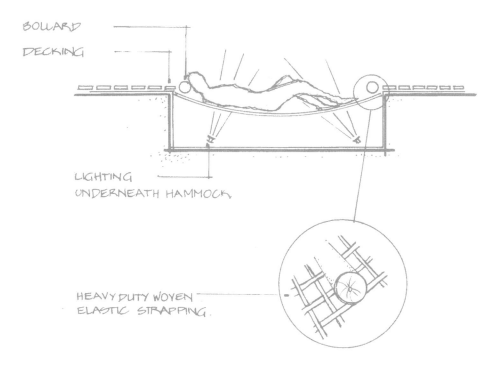

BOLLARD

DECKING

LIGHTING
UNDERNEATH HAMMOCK

HEAVY DUTY WOVEN
ELASTIC STRAPPING.

It's not hard to spot that I love the look of metal and wood together. Man-made alongside organic is far and away my favourite combination of materials. Timber and metal are contemporary and classic all at once and when brought together the resulting piece doesn't need dressing up so it retains an air of wholeness and simplicity. They are so very different, that a marvellous balance occurs so I feature them a lot in my custom-made furniture.

Metals that are ideal for outside include marine-grade aluminium (cast or extruded), and the top-notch finish of stainless steel. Avoid mild steel unless you are deliberately after an ageing or rusted look. It should be powder-coated or galvanised and you must cap the bottom of the object because whatever it sits on (pavers, stone, etc.) will rub back the surface so the steel will eventually corrode and bleed rusty streaks.

I tend to use timbers like tallow-wood, ironbark, teak, cedar, turpentine, kwila and treated pine, but take note that they must all be looked after to some extent. Shellacs, sealers and estapols give strong protection but they lock in the moisture so the wood may eventually crack or chip and you'll have to sand it back and start all over again. I prefer to feed the wood with an oil like tongue oil or teak oil (a pre-boiled product without impurities) which is thin enough to penetrate the grains and nourish the wood while still letting it breathe.

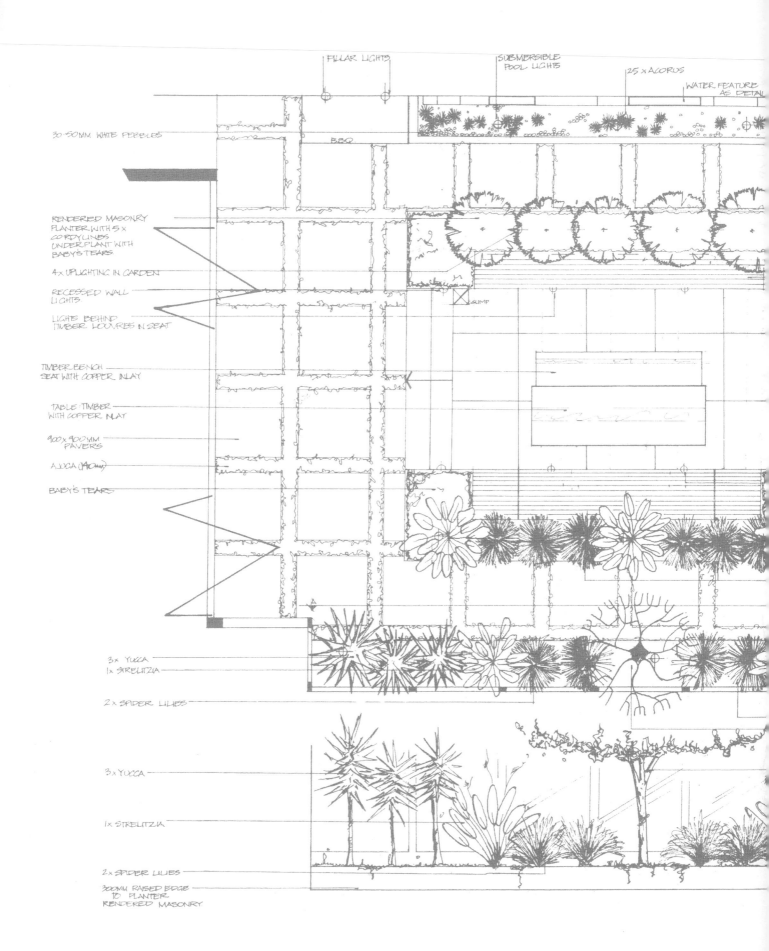

PILLAR LIGHTS

SUBMERSIBLE POOL LIGHTS

25 x ACORUS

WATER FEATURE AS DETAIL

30-50MM WHITE PEBBLES

B.B.Q.

RENDERED MASONRY PLANTER WITH 5 x CORDYLINES UNDERPLANT WITH BABY'S TEARS.

4 x UPLIGHTING IN GARDEN

RECESSED WALL LIGHTS.

LIGHTS BEHIND TIMBER LOUVRES IN SEAT

TIMBER BENCH SEAT WITH COPPER INLAY

TABLE TIMBER WITH COPPER INLAY

900 x 900MM PAVERS

YUCCA (1400MM)

BABY'S TEARS

SUMP

3 x YUCCA
1 x STRELITZIA

2 x SPIDER LILIES

3 x YUCCA

1 x STRELITZIA

2 x SPIDER LILIES

300MM RAISED EDGE TO PLANTER RENDERED MASONRY.

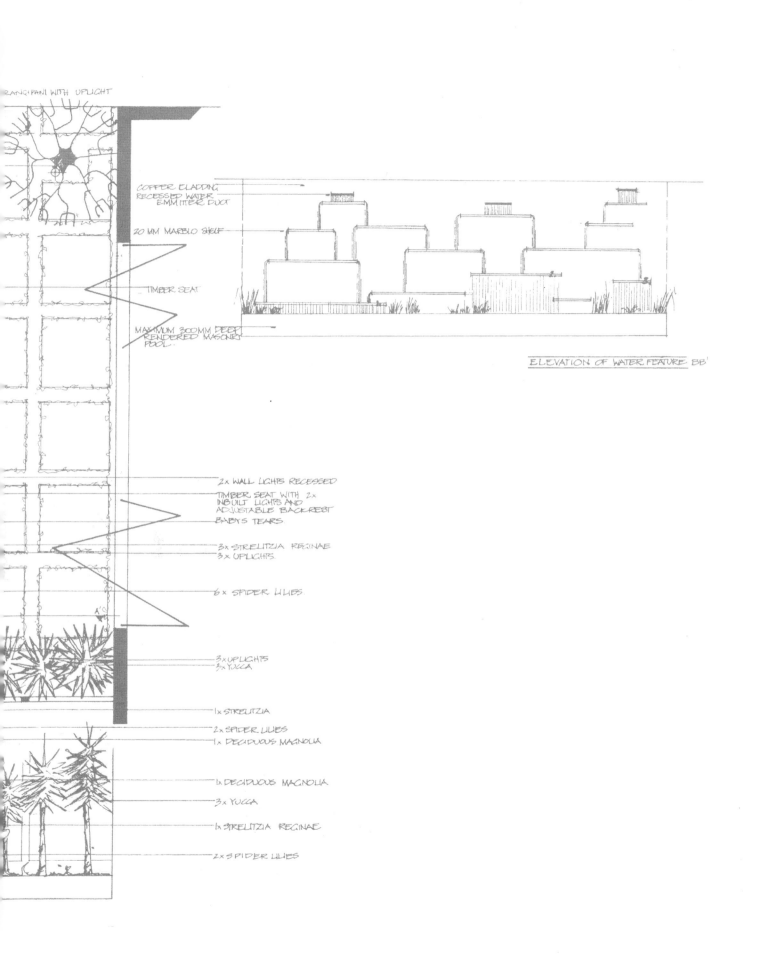

FRANGIPANI WITH UPLIGHT

COPPER CLADDING
RECESSED WATER
EMMITTER DUCT

20 MM MARBLO SHELF

TIMBER SEAT

MAXIMUM 300 MM DEEP
RENDERED MASONRY
POOL.

ELEVATION OF WATER FEATURE BB'

2x WALL LIGHTS RECESSED
TIMBER SEAT WITH 2x
INBUILT LIGHTS AND
ADJUSTABLE BACKREST
BABYS TEARS

3x STRELITZIA REGINAE
3x UPLIGHTS.

6x SPIDER LILIES.

3x UPLIGHTS
3x YUCCA

1x STRELITZIA

2x SPIDER LILIES
1x DECIDUOUS MAGNOLIA

1x DECIDUOUS MAGNOLIA

3x YUCCA

1x STRELITZIA REGINAE

2x SPIDER LILIES

THIS BRIGHT, AIRY balcony needed lots of greenery to interrupt the stark white lines of the base structure. An elevated spa takes full advantage of the tranquil outlook of treetops and sky, while bathers are protected from the wind with a clear glass barrier. To permit all-important drainage, the whole area has a slight incline, so the portable bench seats and tables have been custom-built with adjustable feet to compensate for the slope. Cushions on the planter bench-seat can be removed to make way for a food preparation and serving space when catering for large numbers. The balcony is furnished with elegant stainless steel and timber custom-made furniture (below left), and to complement them, custom-made triangular wall-pots (below right) with ascending containers that hold a cascading display of hardy annuals and succulents.

A MODERN INTERPRETATION of a traditional
Japanese water spout (right). Although usually
made of bamboo, this one is stainless-steel. The
steady flow pours from a bluestone catchment to
the glass pond beneath brimming with plants and a
family of fish. Against the bold, clean lines of a
timber fence on the other side of the balcony,
clumps of ox-eye daisy, flax and Echeveria *are a*
striking contrast in rambling free-form (below).

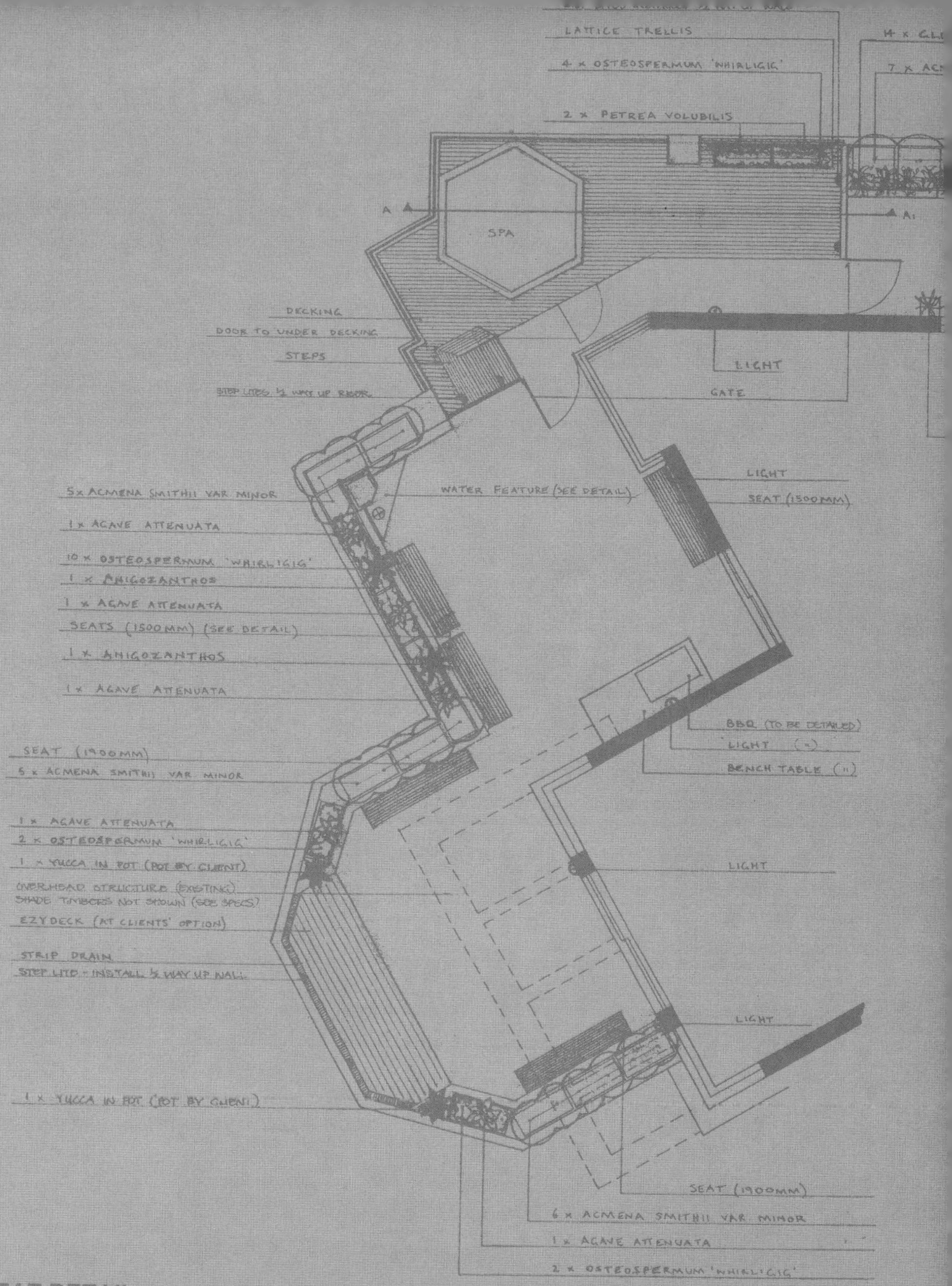

SPA

A   A   A   A₁

DECKING

DOOR TO UNDER DECKING

STEPS

STEP LITES ½ WAY UP RISER

LIGHT

GATE

LIGHT

SEAT (1500MM)

5 x ACMENA SMITHII VAR. MINOR

1 x AGAVE ATTENUATA

10 x OSTEOSPERMUM 'WHIRLIGIG'

1 x ANIGOZANTHOS

1 x AGAVE ATTENUATA

SEATS (1500MM) (SEE DETAIL)

1 x ANIGOZANTHOS

1 x AGAVE ATTENUATA

WATER FEATURE (SEE DETAIL)

BBQ (TO BE DETAILED)

LIGHT   ( )

BENCH TABLE ( )

SEAT (1900MM)

5 x ACMENA SMITHII VAR. MINOR

1 x AGAVE ATTENUATA

2 x OSTEOSPERMUM 'WHIRLIGIG'

1 x YUCCA IN POT (POT BY CLIENT)

OVERHEAD STRUCTURE (EXISTING)
SHADE TIMBERS NOT SHOWN (SEE SPECS)

EZYDECK (AT CLIENTS' OPTION)

STRIP DRAIN

STEP LITE - INSTALL ½ WAY UP WALL

LIGHT

1 x YUCCA IN POT (POT BY CLIENT)

LIGHT

SEAT (1900MM)

6 x ACMENA SMITHII VAR. MINOR

1 x AGAVE ATTENUATA

2 x OSTEOSPERMUM 'WHIRLIGIG'

page
84

SEAT DETAIL
Scale 1:10

10 ~ 35

SATIN PERSPEX PANELS
FIXED AT ALTERNATING
LOCATIONS ON THE 5 SEPARATE
BENCHES SEE A → E

STAINLESS STEEL BOX SECTION
19 x 35MM KAREL TIMBERS

A   B   D   E

50
200
50
150

450

50   50

435

566 TYP

1900
(OR 1500 AS INDICATED ON PLAN
WHERE DISTANCE BETWEEN LEGS TO BE 470MM)

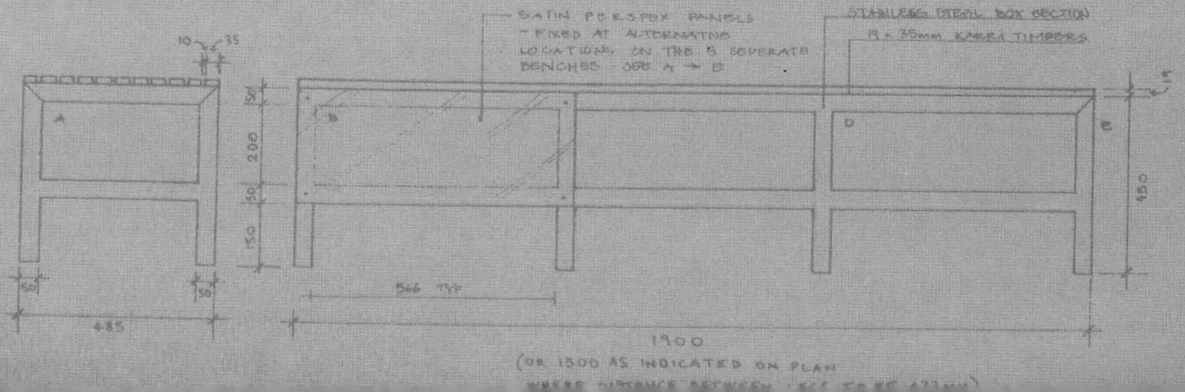

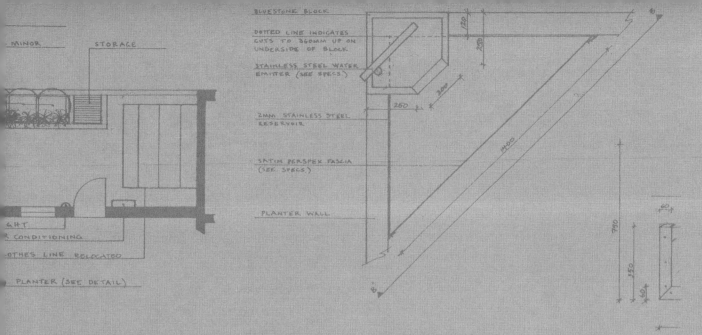

BLUESTONE BLOCK

DOTTED LINE INDICATES
CUTS TO 360MM UP ON
UNDERSIDE OF BLOCK

STAINLESS STEEL WATER
EMITTER (SEE SPECS)

2MM STAINLESS STEEL
RESERVOIR

SATIN PERSPEX FASCIA
(SEE SPECS)

PLANTER WALL

MINOR   STORAGE

GHT
R CONDITIONING
OTHES LINE RELOCATED
PLANTER (SEE DETAIL)

1.2 x 2.4
9   1800
13 1900
13 2000

ON/ ELEVATION AA

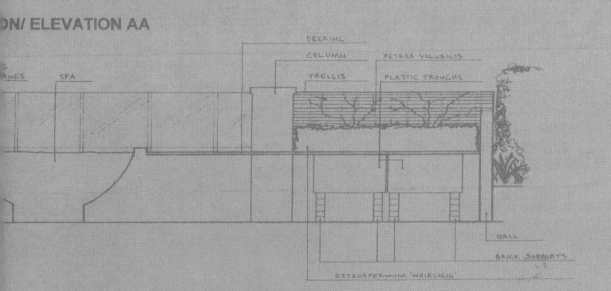

DECKING

COLUMN   PETREA VOLUBILIS

TRELLIS   PLASTIC TROUGHS

NES   SPA

WALL

BRICK SUPPORTS

OSTEOSPERMUM 'WHIRLIGIG'

BROMELIAD PLANTER
Scale 1:10

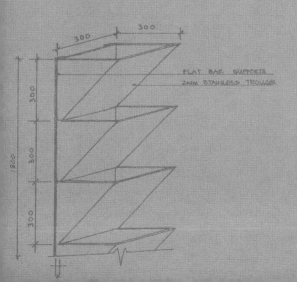

300   300

FLAT BAR SUPPORTS
2MM STAINLESS TROUGHS

PLANT SCHEDULE

BOTANICAL NAME	COMMON NAME	SIZE	QTY.
Acmena smithii var. minor	Lilly Pilly	25L	23
Agave attenuata	Agave	45L	5
Anigozanthos 'Bush Dawn'	Kangaroo Paw	8IN	2
Osteospermum 'Whirligig'	Whirligig Ox-Eye Daisy	6IN	18
Clivea miniata	Clivea	6IN	14
Petrea volubilis	Purple Wreath	8IN	2
Guzmania (cv with burgundy in leaves)	Bromeliad	8IN	6
Yucca elephantipes	Yucca	45L	2

CONTAINMENT

Customised planters are great for filling small or awkward spaces or simply because you want something totally original. I have commissioned fabricators to build planters out of stainless steel, copper, marine-grade aluminium, zinc, plastic and resin, but there are impressive new products appearing on the market every day. Recently I was blown away by some fantastic angular zinc pots from Paris and a couple of thick white plastic urns from Italy that made a stunning focal point in an ultra-hip inner-city courtyard.

If your choice is a permeable substance like reconstituted sandstone, terracotta, concrete, stone or brickwork, be aware that they are porous and will heat up and suck all the moisture and nutrients from the soil – in effect, competing with the plant. This can be overcome by having the surface glazed, so it is less porous and no longer leaches the soil.

When you purchase from the manufacturer, check there are drainage holes in the base – you'd be amazed how many of them neglect this. Make sure the container is large enough for the amount of soil needed to sustain the plant, and if the plant has a large canopy, the pot should be heavily anchored by the weight of the earth or the wind will tip it over.

Design with shapes when you're choosing your foliage: tall and elongated, squat and robust, spiky, feathery, fleshy – think about its

ECO TIP

Any receptacle – and I do mean any – can be adapted into a planter. Become a scavenger like me and you'll look at back sheds, council dumps and hard rubbish days with entirely new eyes. Recycling materials is not only positive from an environmental point of view, but you may also unearth a unique work of 'found art' which infuses tremendous character and personality into your outdoor room. Old metal rubbish bins, tyre parts and discarded wine barrels are just some of the so-called waste materials that have been reclaimed and restored to become quirky, clever and inspiring conversation pieces.

impact on the overall effect. A shrub or small tree that needs a lot of water and fertilizer will struggle in a pot, so go for hardy varieties like flaxes, *Lomandra longifolia*, arum lilies, *Dietes*, yuccas, dracaenas, cacti and succulents, and any of the palms. Also think about which part of the plant is the most attractive: do you want the foliage to be eye height or would you prefer to look down on a canopy of leaves? This will be determined by the size of the container so make sure the pot fits the plant.

PLANTS WITH STRONG shapes work well in containers. Succulents are often a great choice, particularly these spiky agaves. Aloes (centre) or Kalanchoe (right), while Canna 'Tropicana', with its more traditional leaf shape and burnished copper hue, makes an arresting contrast plant.

CONTAINERS
inspiration

Please don't expect the same soil to feed a plant forever. When re-potting, you need to carefully pull the plant out, gently loosen up the root ball, add fresh potting mix and settle it again. Potting mixes have a world of nutritious additives these days: water-saving crystals, slow-release fertilizer, wetting agents, drainage aids and trace elements. The health of your pot plant depends almost entirely on what goes into this mix so don't skimp by settling for the cheaper brands.

It's always a good idea to twist pots around every two to three weeks so sun reaches all parts of the plant and you maintain a healthy, even growth. And the pot should be elevated at least 20mm off the ground so it can drain freely and be easily hosed under. You can use anything you like for this but a couple of pebbles or small stones make sturdy little pedestals and they don't cost a cent.

BITS AND PIECES

Colour and ornamentation are as important for the outside as for the inside, and here's a good way to start thinking about the choices you'll make. Walk through the house observing your fabrics, pictures, the shapes of chairs and vases, jewellery and light fittings. Most of these things can be interpreted in some way for an outdoor setting and adapted to endure the elements. Style-wise, this makes the passage from inside to out a far more seamless transition and promotes a feeling of harmony and completion.

The market for outdoor furniture and equipment is booming. Every luxury, it seems, is catered for, from state-of-the-art sound systems to projection gear for home cinema. I'm all for bringing technology outside but take care not to go overboard: an excess of noisy diversions like television, video and computer games can destroy the unique ambiance of an outdoor space. Focus instead on integrating those little indulgences that lend themselves to a natural environment, like a hammock to rock away a lazy afternoon or a handsome stone chess set for marathon family tournaments.

A SIMPLE, SOLID wooden bench performs well in a busy garden (left). WITH AN EVER-INCREASING array of new furniture styles and materials on the market, the traditional timber bench seat (centre left) remains a fine choice for positions such as this one submerged in a verdant bank of Teucrium. BUILT-IN FURNITURE CAN give you flexibility: rope handles are the only things that give away the large and very useful storage space within this bench (centre right). AN INTENSE SPLASH of colour (right) demands attention and soft, bulky padding invites comfort and repose.

WORKING WITH RATHER than against this
rolling landscape, a pontoon trail of 'mini-
platforms' rises up with the land to serve as
lookout points, then drops down with the fall of
the land providing stepping-stones to cross a small
stream. Moving back towards the house, the path
steps up to a retaining wall and resolves itself in a
daybed that can be cushioned for a snooze in the
sun or just perched upon for a contemplative
breather (below left). Because there was a lot going
on at ground level, it was important to provide a
vertical contrast to balance things up. Large
upright ornamental timbers were placed at random
intervals (below right) and suddenly the garden
took on a whole new, almost monumental
dimension.

TIMBER AND STONE are a pleasant tactile contrast and offer visual diversity as the eye picks its way along the track. Edging this property is a belt of dense bushland so the pontoon trail eventually peters off into the landscape beyond like stepping-stones into the wilderness.

inspiration
FURNISHINGS

for art's sake

Art is such a personal thing, but whatever your taste, I can't emphasise enough how pivotal an art piece can be in placing your individual stamp on an outdoor room. It enhances your feeling of pride and ownership and brings character and personality to the space. You might choose a dry sculpture or a custom-built water feature, you could construct an arrangement of timber on the wall, a mosaic design on the floor or paint a mural on the fence – the possibilities are endless.

If you're having trouble settling on a medium, I would suggest that stone sculpture works stunningly just about everywhere. Classic and timeless, this ancient material radiates a solid immortality that gives the garden a sense of longevity and eternal character. I have long been awed by the monolithic stone circles like Stonehenge and Avebury that dot the English countryside. They are inspiring on a purely aesthetic level but are deeply spiritual, too. Scottish artist Andy Goldsworthy is someone whose work I admire enormously. He is celebrated for imposing startling contemporary designs on a wide range of organic materials and erecting them in vast natural landscapes. This is the essence of what I strive to do in my work every day.

The best advice I can give you is to follow your gut instinct. I can't lead you in any one direction because I truly believe that art should be a reflection of yourself, but perhaps this will help: my most adored personal piece of art is my Yogi. A simple wooden sculpture of a man crouched into a ball, he comes with me every time I move house and is one of the few possessions that I'll never part with. He always looks so peaceful, so well rounded, so symmetrical and yet so solid … to me he symbolises what I struggle to be every day as a person.

I hope you find your own Yogi.

'AS LONG AS YOU CHOOSE WISELY,
A TREE CAN BE THE BEST SCULPTURE YOU EVER
INVEST IN ... AN EVER-CHANGING ART PIECE
WITH ITS OWN SCULPTURAL AGENDA.'

CHAPTER FOUR THE
KITCHEN
FEEDING AND FEASTING

Laughter, conversation, sharing, nurturing: these are all things I associate with cooking and eating outdoors. Food is a huge social magnet. Families and friends congregate around the table in anticipation of being fed, building relationships and celebrating the joys of togetherness – and it all seems that little bit more special when experienced in a natural environment.

Isn't it funny how food seems to taste better outside? I like to think it's a primal memory buried deep in our psyches that dates back to a time when our ancient ancestors cooked and ate around an open fire. Whatever the reason, people of all cultures continue to be drawn to the flames and I get a buzz every time I see a tiny inner-city balcony almost completely taken up by the prized barbecue. Such dedication!

Let's not forget that it's great for male bonding: once blokes step out the door and grab the tongs it's suddenly okay to cook. But these days the outdoor kitchen is not just about the ubiquitous barbie. More and more of my clients are asking for the same amenities outside as they have in their indoor kitchens and I'm more than happy to oblige. Being outside separates you somehow from normality, giving you a kind of holiday from the everyday. What luxury to be fully set up when you're cooking outdoors. I promote whenever I can the novelty of having everything at your fingertips.

THE GREAT AUSSIE OBSESSION

So many choices in outdoor cooking facilities are available now, there really is no excuse for an ugly piece of equipment which looks awkward and out of place. If you customise your barbecue and work to blend it in with the theme, it becomes part of the garden and not just an afterthought, so respect it as you would a key piece of furniture. I'll generally select the model in close consultation with the client and purchase it without a stand. Then together we take the time to choose appropriate cladding and cover it in a way that echoes the style of the whole room. Apart from aesthetics, customising your barbecue also saves space, allowing for benches on either side and cupboard space beneath.

A few dos and don'ts about positioning: never seat diners so close that they might be spattered by fat or have smoke billowing in their faces. Keep it as far away from windows as possible and ensure that the hotplates are well lit for night-time cook-outs. At the same time don't place the culinary action away from the sitting area. It's important for the chef to participate and, let's face it, food preparation is a wonderful conversational tool. A big part of the pleasure of the outdoor cooking and eating experience is to make sure everyone's involved, either helping set up the meal or mucking in with the cleanup.

Try to place your cooker beneath a wall that will act as a barrier in case things go wrong gas-wise, and if your gas bottles are exposed at all, make sure doors are locked when children are around. (Rule number one: gas and kids don't mix!) And while you're at it, check that sharp utensils and any breakables are under lock and key, just as they would be in the inside kitchen.

A DINING TABLE emerges smoothly from the timber deck and then vanishes into a single plane, freeing up precious space. Designed by Patio team-member David Vago, this small courtyard off an inner-city terrace is full of great solutions to the outdoor dining dilemma. Once the table is raised into place, the surrounding deck is transformed to become in situ bench seating with rattan cushions trimmed in Chinese silk. A shallow rill of water embraces a portion of the dining area and, softly illuminated with spills of light, it becomes a velvety liquid carpet when night falls.

AH – THE BARBECUE in action! This unit was purchased without a stand and installed with brick and timber surrounds, blending seamlessly with the overall theme. High barriers on two sides act as safety walls, and plenty of bench space puts condiments and implements within easy reach. Best of all is the proximity of chef to diners, which allows the free flow of conversation and ensures the tantalising aroma of food being prepared whets everyone's appetite.

Stainless steel and sealed granite are a popular choice for benchtops because they require minimal grout and their non-porous properties guarantee that foodstuffs won't stain them. When not in use, these surfaces can double as stands for small pieces of sculpture or other ornamentation. Splashbacks to the rear of the cooking plate are a must as well as being a fine opportunity for accent colour. Fix a shelf along the splashback and you have condiments and utensils within easy reach while you prepare the meal. Utilities like sinks and fridges are easy enough to install and, as for outdoor cookware, the sky's the limit. Basically, if your crockery and implements can withstand the punishment dished out in an average kitchen, then they can withstand whatever the outdoor elements throw at them, too.

WHERE THE HEARTH IS

It's a great feeling being outside in the wind and weather on a chilly afternoon but you're snuggled up and warm as toast. Outdoor heaters seem to be everywhere these days, particularly in those parts of the country with a cooler climate. For smaller spaces like courtyards and balconies, wall-mounted heaters are safe and very effective. Then there are the hooded umbrella-style heaters which have really taken off in the last few years because they are safe, self-sufficient with their own gas bottles, and easy to move around. You'll see them outside cafes and restaurants in the winter months, bringing in the business and lots of cosy customers. It's just another part of controlling your environment out there by customising it to suit yourself. The more comfortable you make your outdoor room for every circumstance, the more you're going to use it.

GATHER ROUND

Most outdoor rooms and courtyards are geometrical by nature so I prefer the table to be geometric, too. For this reason, you'll see the majority of the tables in my garden designs are rectangular, allowing for the greatest diversity in seating arrangement. Benches are another story altogether and you can really go to town experimenting with voluptuous curves, but tables need to fit into L-shaped seating designs so that you can cater for large numbers if need be.

NEUTRAL-COLOURED WALLS are a calm background for randomly criss-crossed stands of Black Bamboo with its unmistakable clumps of massed foliage and smatterings of fragile leaves.

In the interests of comfort, benches should be 450mm to 600mm wide and 420mm to 550mm high. When you place the table, there needs to be no more than 150mm between the edge of the table and the edge of the bench. Any further away and diners have to lean in too far to reach their plates; any closer and it starts to get a bit tight squeezing in and out, which is especially problematic for the less mobile among us.

AN EDIBLE GARDEN

There are few things more satisfying than being able to reach out and pluck your own ingredients straight from the soil. Growing food and flavourings is easy and you don't need much room: even the smallest flat can have a mini herb garden. Start with a humble window box on a sunny sill, fill it with chives, basil, coriander, dill and parsley, feed it regularly and change the soil every six months or so, and you're in business.

For larger spreads it's all about location. The bed or planter needs to be in the right spot – out of the wind but with plenty of sun – and it should be raised to a good height so you don't have to bend down far to tend to it. A smorgasbord of vegetables planted in clever formation will produce a brilliant ornamental mass that easily rivals any flower display.

ECO TIP

As attractive and welcoming as wood burners can be, sadly they are no good for the planet because wood smoke is high on the list of greenhouse emissions. They're not so good for the human respiratory system either, because the high particle emission is known to trigger asthma attacks. Your best bet is to go for gas heaters and take comfort in the fact they are a clean and cost-effective burn.

I love clusters of curly endive, cherry tomatoes, chillies (especially the Thai varieties) and basil all crowded together in a glorious edible mess. Clumps of herbs make neat, frilly borders and spread rapidly into fragrant groundcovers. Garden beds framed by rosemary hedges look fantastic, with the added bonus that when you brush the leaves as you pass, a marvellously fresh and subtle scent is released.

If you're thinking about including edibles in your plant landscape, there are some definite stand-outs that look as good as they taste. Pineapples are an arresting accent plant with their striking architectural form, while passionfruits are brilliant for climbing and screening (*Passiflora edulis* will fruit more if you train it to climb laterally). Cumquats bring forth gleaming little orange orbs and hold their shape well, especially when they're hedged or topiaried. You can't go wrong with the tangy scent of lemons and oranges and the dwarf varieties grow exceptionally well in pots. Apples have a delicate blossom and lustrous crop and pears with their distinctive shapely fruit prosper in cooler climates. Strawberries are a sweet and abundant groundcover, and pumpkins and zucchinis thrive in hot spaces. I've always had a soft spot for edible flowers, too. My mum sprinkles bright splashes of marigold in her legendary salads, and my grandma in Sri Lanka used to slip nasturtium leaves in my sandwiches for a little extra spice.

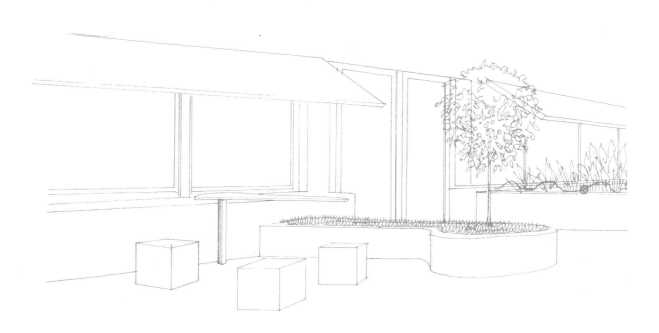

SKETCHES ARE GREAT for identifying whether different shapes will work in the space. Here we see how kidney-shaped (above), oval (top right) and linear furnishings play a dominant role in each of these outdoor rooms.

SURFBOARD SWINGING TABLE: MARINE PLY 1700×600 MM
SUNSET FLAME AND MARITIME HARMONY

3 × PAINTED TIMBER BLOCK SEATS 450×
450×450 MM

MINI-WALL DOUBLE SKIN TO
RENDER AS A
BENCH SEAT

8 × GREEN FLEXI-TEK PAVERS

-BRIGHT YELLOW
-SUNSET FLAME
-MARITIME HARMONY

MICHELLIA FIGO STANDARD
UNDERPLANT WITH MINI-
MONDO LAWN.

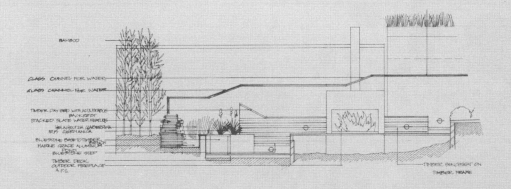

BAMBOO

GLASS CHANNEL FOR WATER
GLASS CHANNEL FOR WATER

TIMBER DAY BED WITH ACCEPTABLE
BACKGREEN
STACKED SLATE WATER FEATURE
HAKONECHLOA MACRA/IRIS
IRIS GERMANICA

BLUESTONE BASE TO TIMBER
MARINE GRADE ALUMINIUM
BLUESTONE STEP

TIMBER DECK
OUTDOOR FIREPLACE
AFS

TIMBER BENCHSEAT ON
TIMBER FRAME

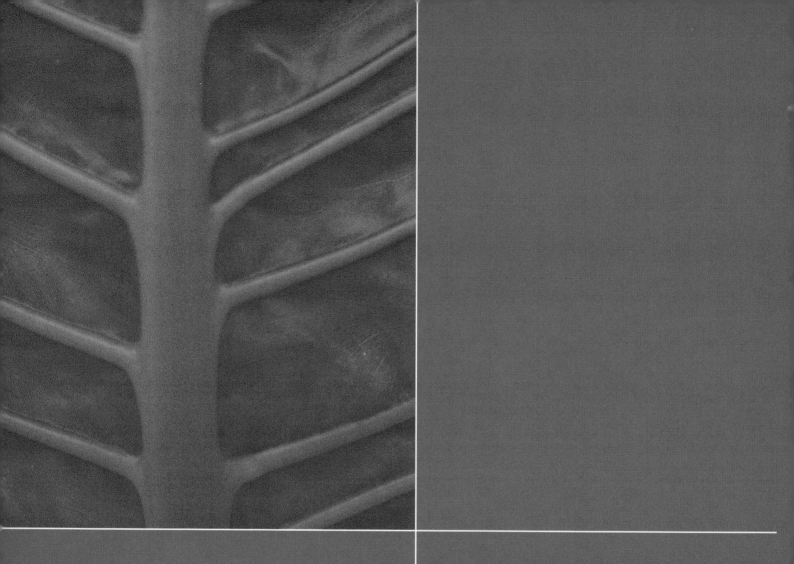

COLOUR
inspiration

into bloom

You might not think it, but I absolutely adore flowers. The trouble is, most of the challenges in my work involve large-scale architectural constructions and the smaller decorative touches come long after I have left the scene. Given the space, the sun and the time, I will jump at the chance to get stuck into the floral side of things. In the past I've had the privilege of designing landscapes for several country gardens and I love the freedom of playing with different forms of foliage and thoroughly satisfying my green thumb.

In the outdoor room, a shapely pot or urn looks wonderful filled with masses of dazzling colour. Anything with strappy, upright foliage is good: November lilies and day lilies make an arresting statement, as does *Strelitzia reginae* (Bird of Paradise) whose structure makes it one of the best accent plants for a courtyard space. Don't forget bulbs and the joy they bring, particularly to children. Vivid clumps of daffodils and clouds of perfumed jonquils are a glorious annual event and the exquisite cups of tulip flowers are the embodiment of spring.

GREVILLIA SERICEA *(top left)*, Banksia spinulosa *(rop right)*, Strelitzia reginae *var.* juncea *(above)*, Aechmea fasciata *(facing page)*.

CHAPTER FIVE THE BATHROOM
ULTIMATE CLEAN

Do you remember the first time you went skinny-dipping? For me the occasion was at an isolated billabong in north-western Australia when I was nine years old. There was nobody else around apart from me and some mates so we dared each other to lose the swimmers and all jumped in together. At first I felt incredibly exposed, but then I started to relax and gradually became suffused with a strange kind of energy. There's something amazing about moving through water with nothing but the sky to cover you, feeling very much a part of the natural world.

Of course, there aren't too many opportunities in the city to take an outdoor dip au naturel. I associate that kind of experience with holidays – an empty beach, private spa or secluded waterhole. How fantastic to be able to recreate that sensation in your own home: soaking in a hot tub on a cool evening, surrounded by lush plants and a velvety sky above, staring at the moon … makes you smile just thinking about it!

Then there's the experience of bathing with a friend or four. In my mind, eating together is a lot like bathing together. Just as food is a reason to congregate and build relationships, so is water a relaxing place to gather and talk and share. In ancient Rome, the public baths were important social centres where business was conducted, friendships made, and news and gossip exchanged. In this country of water-lovers, I think it's a great shame that a culture of communal bathing never took off, but an outdoor bathroom must surely be the next best thing.

rain room

'I'll never ever forget my first trip to Bali when I signed up for a massage in a 'rain room'. For close to an hour my body was gently pummelled until I tingled all over, then the masseur stepped out and activated a system of sprinklers criss-crossing the ceiling.

The room began to rain!

The delight of that afternoon has stayed with me and made me determined to find ways of reproducing a similar kind of experience for my clients whenever budget allows.'

SHOWER POWER

Time and again I've installed an outdoor shower and the client will say to me months later that they use it far more often than their indoor facilities. So look out – you might get addicted!

The beauty of it is that you don't need a lot of space. As long as your walls are high enough, the only other basic requirements are a shower rose and adequate drainage that empties into the stormwater system. If you prefer to feel more enclosed, there's everything from folding glass shutters to a mass of upright screening plants to hinder prying eyes. Much depends on the prevailing theme but I would try to use, as always, a natural material which is more tactile and welcoming against bare skin.

The floor for the shower area must be able to withstand blasts of water and prolonged periods of dampness. A series of treated timber dowel batons fixed in a row gives adequate grip and feels good under wet feet. Pavers should have a matt finish and be slip-resistant. A slab of porous stone is fine, as long as it is in a position where it can dry in the sun. If polished or honed stone is the main floor surface in your outdoor room, the shower area must be completely surrounded and separated from the rest so that water isn't walked across the floor or doesn't accidentally drain into the living area and make it a slippery hazard zone.

As for the green screen, any water-loving plants – such as papyrus – will thrive in the moist atmosphere.

BUBBLE-TUBS AND MINI OCEANS

Once upon a time spas were a true luxury item, found only in the homes of the very rich and the very decadent. Now anyone can install their own kit spa: the plumbing is included so the cladding and surrounds are all you have to worry about. Decking is my preferred surface because it's non-slip and maintains an even temperature as well as being soft on the feet and beautiful to lie on with bare skin.

If you are fortunate enough to have a view from your outdoor room, position the tub or spa so that whoever is using it can take full advantage of the natural vista. By the same token, if there is no outlook to exploit, then create one – a special feature for the eye to rest upon while the body enjoys a long, bubbly soak.

Swimming pools are the supreme example of bringing your holiday back home, symbolically recreating the seaside in a domestic domain. Like all other elements of the outdoor room, a pool can be dressed up to become the main focus for indulgent activities. Recently I saw a pool that typified how a simple addition to the pool area can make it look extravagant and luxurious. Deliberately sunk beside a well-established avocado tree, the deck was built around the foliage so you could just reach up and pick the fruit from its lush, laden branches. Talk about indulgent!

When I design pools, I always aim to include enticements for people to linger once they've had their swim. The wet edge is an innovation I've begun to use, where a shallow indent runs along the entire length of one side. A sheet of water gently sluices over the lip, cooling sunbathers with a sensual trickle so they feel they are still immersed in the main body of water.

THE PILLAR WATER feature consists of random-split slabs of grey slate. Water emerges from a slit near the top of the pillar and slides silently down the pearly grey surface to replenish the channel beneath. The narrow rill that embraces this tile expanse instantly cools the space and provides a flicker of constant movement. Light timber pontoons lie across the rill, allowing access to the bench seats either side of the pillar where the sitter might choose to dangle hot feet in the delicious cool. A fine finishing touch is the glass mosaic edge of muted blue-grey tiles.

THIS LARGE COURTYARD is constantly in use so it's important for the owners to be able to clear the decks for the next activity. The barbecue (left) is mobile so can be stored in the corner, and there is an icebox beneath the tiled benches. Other benches conceal the entire water-filter system. It's a canine paradise – and pretty good for the human occupants, too! With a couple of energetic water-loving pets like Stoli and Tiger, the owners were delighted with this shallow dog-safe mini-pool running along the boundary-line (below).

HIGH TIMBER WALLS snuggle up to a bank of dense foliage with enough privacy for an unscreened shower which is used far more frequently than the home-owners expected. And who can blame them? The wooden deck feels great underfoot (with spaces between the slats for good drainage), there's lots of lush greenery to enjoy, and the timber screen provides sufficient privacy while still revealing a pleasing view of the garden beyond.

Any pool will dominate a backyard, so great care should be taken with its visual presentation, no matter what size. Turquoise is inevitably associated with tropical locations so it's a great colour for pool interiors, but I've seen black, slate and even red pool interiors that look magnificent in gardens with a strong contemporary flavour. Just remember that the darker the pool colour is, the smaller it will look, and in those cases where there is a lot of high shadowy foliage around it, the inky depths can look positively forbidding.

There's no avoiding the ugly accompaniment of plastic coils and boxes of filter gear, but I've come to see that disguising the pool cleaning system is an opportunity to introduce interesting new structures into the outdoor room. Think of the pump housing as a striking level change: a ready-made stand for pots brimming with lush plant life, its sides perhaps festooned with creepers.

The texture of the finish will often be a big factor in determining the amount of maintenance you'll need to keep your pool sparkling clean. Pebblecrete finishes look natural and feel pleasant underfoot but debris can settle and stubbornly cling to them. Smoother surfaces like epoxy paints on rendered concrete are low maintenance because they don't attract grime and are easy to vacuum. As a bonus, concrete can be dressed up with a continuous panel of mosaic tile on the skim-line which, when colour-matched, ties in with the general theme of the outdoor room.

ECO TIP

The design of the showerhead is crucial to the amount of water used. Compared to a conventional showerhead, the AAA-rated water-saving rose will consume 52 litres less water during an eight-minute shower – that's a saving of 18 980 litres a year!

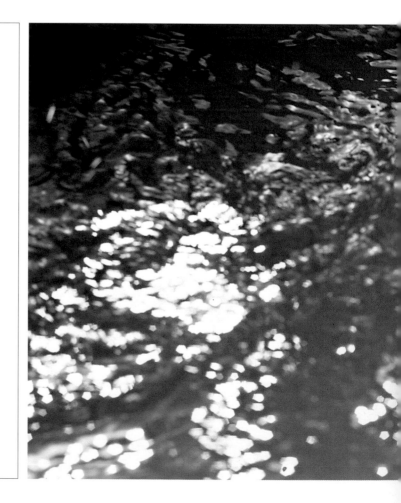

A DENSE STAND of bamboo makes a great screen to protect your privacy in an outdoor bathroom. Here you can see that with stripy bamboo (centre) the beauty is in the detail. There's no doubt about it: when it comes to patterns, nature wins hands down every time. Another beautiful – and rare – bamboo is Giant Timber Bamboo (Dendrocalamopsis oldhamii, *overleaf*). And when it comes to sun protection, nature also provides. This giant elephant's ear (Alocasia macrorrhiza, *right*) is an attractive and effective sunshade.

'HALF THE PLEASURE
OF THE OUTDOOR ROOM IS
NURTURING WHAT'S IN IT.'

a fantasy...

One day the outdoor room will be a standard
part of every Australian home, just like the
kitchen or living room is now. I can almost
picture the real estate advertisements in the
Saturday papers:

*'Solid brick family home comprising three spacious bedrooms, family
room, formal dining, bathroom, kitchen and meals area, laundry, fully
functioning outdoor room and landscaped garden plus OSP ...'*

*'Two-bedroom apartment, spacious lnge and dining with north-facing
balcony room and fountain, eat-in kitchen, sep laundry, central htg
and LUG ...'*

*'Beautifully located 2BR Victorian conceals 3 bright liv/din spaces
including outdoor room with kitchenette and tub ...'*

A CONTEMPORARY VERSION *of the backyard tub. Black-stained timber, offset with polished pebbles, leads up to the bath, where the bather can lie back and study cloud formations for hours on end (or at least until the water goes cold). A mulberry-coloured curved wall takes care of nosy passers-by, with a tall screen of copper strips and bamboo poles painted a luscious tomato-red to provide visual relief against its solid expanse. In the foreground are mounds of glossy* Hebe, *while the lawn section (below) descends in curved terraces, held in place by copper strips that echo the dominating screen at the rear.*

Clients often come to me with an existing pool that they want to look new again. Merely surrounding the area with a new surface (like timber decking) and extending a length of coping down into the water will transform it completely.

And finally, whether you are renovating or building anew, make sure the surfaces surrounding the pool echo the surfaces in the outdoor room. Too many materials create visual boxes, so keep it simple and the pool will not look separated from the rest of the garden.

The old claw-footed tub doesn't require any kind of barrier but spas and pools that are permanently filled with water must be fenced off by law. Check with your local council for the specifics, but generally fences must have self-closing doors with locks or latches that are too high for children to reach and need to be at least a metre away from all other climbable constructions and boundaries. Any lateral slats or bars within the fence structure are illegal.

Fence costs vary, with the frameless glass barrier hovering at the top of the range and the standard powder-coated aluminium bars one of the more popular cheap options. Both fulfil the safety obligations and both look good in the right situation.

To avoid the feeling that you are 'caged' by the fence, dot plants around the perimeter. Any Australian species that survive the so-called front line salt tolerant areas (ie coastal) are better for around pools, including *Scaevola* and *Westringia*.

SETTING THE SCENE

Now for the finishing touches. There are so many simple, cheap and effective ways to promote an atmosphere of pleasure and repose around water. Candles need no justification: they are a compulsory addition to any meditative or romantic situation and you can never have too many. The delicate scent of incense or oil burners, the golden flicker of an ornate lantern, the melodic tinkle of wind chimes all foster a restful ambiance. For a truly indulgent bathing experience, sprinkle aromatic flower petals on the surface (try rose petals, geranium petals or my all-time favourite, frangipani).

inspiration
BATHROOM

WATER IS AN *all-pervading presence in this beautiful harbourside home, and what better way to introduce the theme than this dramatic entranceway with its lush stand of* Strelitzia nicolai *on one side and a glassy lap pool on the other. A quick after-swim rinse in the poolside shower, and bathers are ready to move on to the spa bath out the back with a spectacular uninterrupted view down to the sea.*

WATER FEATURE
IT'S ELEMENTARY

If you want to create a garden that is truly whole, you must include as many natural elements as possible. Again, this is an idea that stems from the Japanese tradition of a garden as a miniature landscape, and you'd have to agree no landscape is complete without an ocean, a river or a glittering ribbon of water running through. This is just one of the reasons why I believe it's so important to have some kind of liquid source in your outdoor space.

When people ask me why I am so passionate about water, I just say, 'Me and twenty million others!' Australians are predominantly coastal dwellers. Whether we live in sight of the ocean or not, we are inevitably drawn to the water.

It's just our way. We choose to have our holidays there, our weekends, we go there to escape, to unwind, to regroup. Is it any wonder then that more and more of us seek to bring some kind of symbolic reminder of this experience into our personal living spaces?

I always encourage my clients to include water (most don't need much convincing), and it invariably ends up being the prime sensual focus, stimulating sight, sound, touch, smell and even taste (if you want to go that far). Cool, clear moving liquid refreshes the soul, it's a superb tool for relaxation and is perfectly in keeping with my philosophy on what the outdoor room should provide.

THE JOURNEY

Building a water feature is a science and it can be a major structural operation so the decision to include one needs to come early in the piece. First you must establish if there's an appropriate place for it. Will it be seen to its maximum advantage? Do you want a single jet or a system of meandering waterways to trail around the space like a unifying thread? Will it be incorporated into levels or run beside pathways? Is there a vantage point that allows it to be seen from inside as well?

Don't be discouraged if your outdoor room seems too small – there's always a place for water. You can run a skin of water down an existing wall, hover an elegant tap over an ornamental basin or install a system of rills around the perimeter. Be aware of the noise factor in a smaller space: loud splashing in close proximity can be very irritating, so avoid long falls of water and keep the pressure down low. On the other hand, the gurgle of running water can be a blessed antidote to the intrusive hum of background urban noise.

Keeping children's safety in mind, I'll usually build the reservoir, cistern or balance tank well out of reach of curious little ones. In the case of exposed water like open streams or cascades, the run will only be 50mm to 60mm deep, so kids can interact without being in any danger.

THERE'S A DISTINCTIVE contemporary flavour in this terrace house, and the aim was to take the feeling outside to the tiny courtyard which opens directly onto the main living room. A feature wall of stucco plasterwork (overleaf) was painted Porter's 'Library Red' to contrast with the white smooth render. Five stainless-steel disc-shaped emitters spurt even jets into the stainless-steel rill, a movement echoed by sprays of Xanthorrhoea *(Grass Tree, right). Pots of* Crassula *and* Kalanchoe *(left) echo the disc shapes with their plump round leaves.*

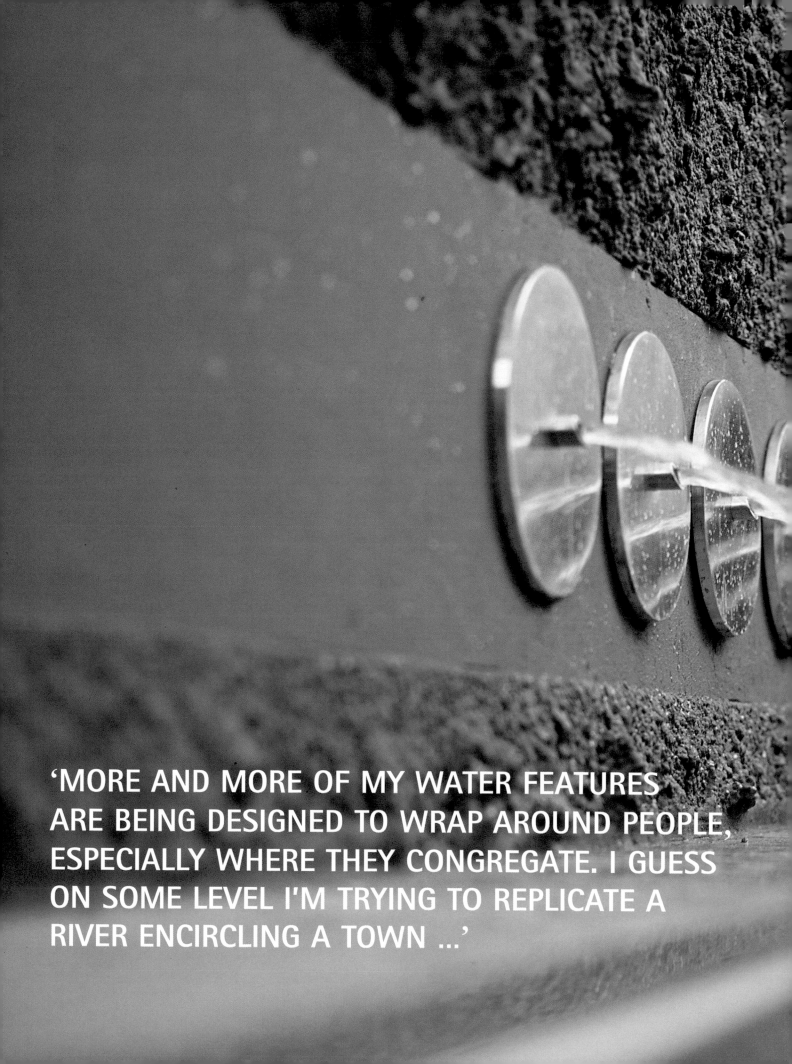

'MORE AND MORE OF MY WATER FEATURES
ARE BEING DESIGNED TO WRAP AROUND PEOPLE,
ESPECIALLY WHERE THEY CONGREGATE. I GUESS
ON SOME LEVEL I'M TRYING TO REPLICATE A
RIVER ENCIRCLING A TOWN ...'

There are some hard and fast rules that apply to all spaces. Water needs sun shining on it for at least part of the day or mosquitoes may converge and breed. It also needs to be protected from drafts and breezes, as wind promotes rapid evaporation and your water levels will soon deplete. The colour of your catchment pond or vessel deserves some careful consideration. A bright, light shade is fine for shallow runs but a more substantial catchment looks great in a darker shade. Not only does it increase the illusion of depth, it also acts as a mirror, reflecting the plant life around it and the sky overhead and it conceals unsightly debris, mould and tannin stains from falling leaves. Finally, keep as much of the mechanics concealed as possible so the eye is drawn to the actual fall of the water and not the place where it ends up. In simple terms, allow the viewer to focus on the journey more than the destination: it's the movement of the water that is exciting.

AQUA INTERRUPTUS

On its own, water seems passive to the naked eye. It only comes alive when it interacts with something, becoming dynamic as it responds to what's around it. I will rarely run water over a surface without some kind of interruption and this is where the interest comes in. The challenge is to ensure that the water doesn't kick off the obstruction and spray outwards; it needs to calmly leave and return to the main surface with smooth ripples, not moisture-guzzling splashes.

Because I design so many water features, I'm always searching for new waterproof materials to work with and new ways to make them interact. Glass, stainless steel, brass, stone, perspex and resin are materials I frequently turn to, and I'm endlessly fascinated by what water does to metals like copper, forcing it to adapt and to age naturally by oxidisation.

IMPORTED FROM TURKEY, this graceful marble basin feature with its elaborate filigree tap is an exotic addition to a shady rustic garden. The visual clincher here is the clever use of colour which sets the contemplative mood. Dark green foliage from next door peeps over the wall to find complementary hues in the deep purple taro plant or Elephant's Ear (Colocasia esculenta 'Black Magic') nestled in the basin. Uniting the palette is the rendered wall painted a soothing slate blue and deliberately distressed so the base material shows through with varying texture and patches of salt damp. The effect is one of timeworn charm, classic design and a hint of faraway places.

THE BRIEF FOR *this major project in the entranceway of an interior design centre was for a natural, free-flowing, safe and unobtrusive installation in breezy neutral tones. Limestone and glass are the base materials: a combination which to my mind works in faultless harmony with the reflective qualities of water, especially when lit up at night.*

SLABS OF BROKEN *limestone sandwiched between broad planes of glass make up the vertical component of the feature. Water rises in a slender channel carved through the centre of each stone 'mountain', seeps down its waved edges and across the rippled stone terraces at the base before finally disappearing in the narrow crack, where it is recycled and begins its journey once more. The whole structure is slightly elevated so people can sit on the rim and dip their fingers in. Children love this 'big pond' and it's perfectly safe for them to interact. I'm a firm believer that you can find inspiration absolutely everywhere. The carved stone mounds in this feature (detail overleaf) came directly from memories of playing with an ant farm when I was a kid. In my travels, I've been lucky enough to see the real thing: dramatic ant-hills towering like metre-high monoliths in the Australian desert. I'm reminded of their haunting beauty and the hive of industriousness within whenever I look at this.*

DO THE RIGHT THING

In these days of shortages and restrictions, water is very much at the forefront of environmental concerns. Every feature will lose a small amount of moisture, but in most cases the water is fully recycled, and water features don't consume water and nutrients as a large plant taking up that same space would. A still body of water has calming, reflective properties

I've seen wonderfully intricate water construc-tions made with branches of driftwood, pieces of pottery and crazy twists of scrap metal, as well as catchments from every conceivable waterproof vessel under the sun. So whatever you do, keep an open mind and be prepared to give anything a go.

GREEN WATER WORLD

I don't think I've ever met a water plant I didn't like. I guess that's why the features that appeal to me most are the ones that use fresh water, replicating wetlands or marshes on a much smaller scale. I like the idea of introducing a body of water where a frog or a fish or a bird can interact – particularly in the middle of a city where a natural oasis is a rare sight.

but generally it's desirable to have a degree of turbulence so the liquid constantly oxygenates, making it fresh and clean. Keep in mind the fact that the slower it moves the less evaporation will occur, and a free-falling cascade will often splash or be carried by the wind, losing precious moisture.

A JAPANESE WATER spout – in stainless-steel
rather than bamboo – spills water into a glass pond
(left). AS NATURAL AS can be, a single plume
bubbles in a shallow bowl carved into a block of
sandstone encircled by nodding leaves (centre).
WATER SPRAYS FROM between overlapping
sheets of cor-ten (right).

These days I'm doing a lot of multi-tiered waterfalls with short drops from level to level. Each catchment is filled with its own miniature eco-system made up of a variety of bog plants like Sedge (*Carex*) and Rush (*Juncus*), bulrush, *Isolepis nodosa* and *Helmholtzia glaberrima* (Stream Lily). They naturally help filter the water, they look great, and some species even discourage mosquitoes.

Other plants that thrive in a watery environment are arum lilies, Louisiana Iris, *Nymphaea*, *Acorus gramineus* and, of course, the ever-versatile papyrus. But I must admit to a huge bias towards the stunning lotus. Every incarnation of this plant looks sensational, from the seed pods to the unopened buds to the bird-like flowers. In fact, I love them so much that the logo for my design business is based on a stylised lotus shape.

A final tip: water plants are generally quite hardy but they will struggle if the water is polluted or if they have been planted too deeply. When too much of the foliage is underwater, the plant is prevented from photosynthesising and it will eventually die.

MAINTAIN THE SPARKLE

Happily, water features are very easy to maintain once they've been installed correctly. Here are some useful trouble-shooting tips.

An OVERFLOW PIPE about 30mm in diameter should be installed in every pond about 20mm above the water surface to prevent overflow and flooding.

AUTOMATIC FLOAT-VALVES are nifty little gadgets available from irrigation suppliers that help keep the water at an even level.

AN AUTHENTIC MOROCCAN design hand-carved in sandstone, this unusual wall-fountain emanates character and charm. A healthy Ficus pumila *(creeping fig) paints the wall behind a deep emerald hue to blend with what is already a very green space. The pond below is edged with bagged brickwork and softened by a cluster of arum lilies. Opening directly onto this view is the master bedroom, so the owners are greeted every new day by this blissful sight.*

FOR PLANTING IN and around water features, or even in damp areas, choose plants that enjoy a moist environment, like this giant elephant's ear (Alocasia macrorrhiza, left). Bromeliads (centre and right) thrive in a moist, humid atmosphere, but need good drainage for their roots.

BIO-FILTER is an innovative new cleaning system which provides a home for good bacteria to work on breaking down the toxins that build up in the water.

RULES AND REGULATIONS vary with different councils around Australia, but generally, a body of water should be no deeper than 300mm or else it must be surrounded by a pool fence.

DISCOURAGE MOSQUITOES by ensuring there is some sort of movement in the water and that sun shines directly on it for part of the day. You can also add salt or chlorine to the mix, and plants like *Helmholtzia glaberrima* are excellent insect turn-offs, too.

TANNIN from fallen leaves will cause discolouration, so avoid planting trees and shrubs close to the basin or pond.

ALONG ONE SIDE of this inner-city terrace, a small, dank, cupboard-like void was transformed into a water-room with a distinctly modern edge to match the stylish interior of the home. Walls were clad in stone, and long vertical glass louvres were fixed at carefully spaced intervals. Discreet emitters dispense a steady stream down the glass panes into a shallow pool below, which is filled with black pebbles that conceal the unsightly pump and pipes.

teamwork

Everyone has the capability to create an exceptional outdoor room. And like any creative enterprise, it's always good to get other people involved once your plans start to take shape. I can't count the number of times I've walked into a garden and immediately picked out things that lend themselves to a theme only to have the owner admit that it had never occurred to them. The simple truth is you can't help but take your own place for granted, especially if you've lived there for a while.

Without my colleagues at Patio, my design concepts would remain just that. They are the ones who spur me on, support my ideas and help provide the technical expertise to make my designs a reality. I'd be lost without these guys – they've been an indispensable touchstone throughout my creative journey.

So don't be afraid to bounce ideas off someone else, whether it be a professional designer or a trusted friend. Remember there really is nothing like a fresh eye: it's easy, it's clever, and it helps you take full advantage of what's right in front of you.

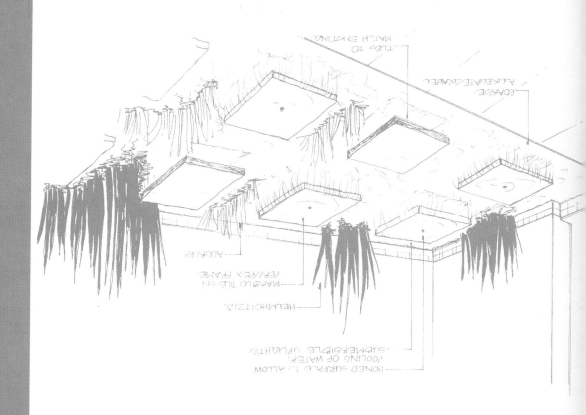

WATER FEATURES

inspiration

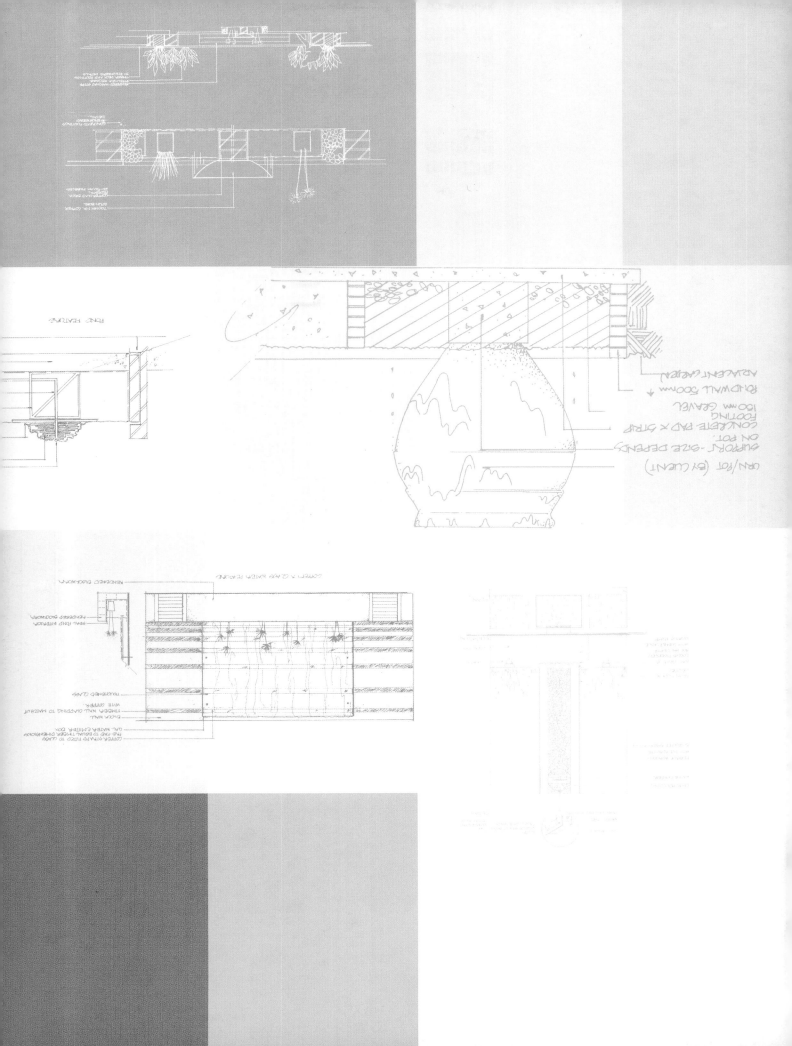

CHAPTER SEVEN LET THERE BE
LIGHT

Well it just goes to show, you can take the boy out of Vegas, but you can't take Vegas out of the boy! For nearly a decade I was based in that glittering city in the heart of the Nevada desert, famous for its frantic nightlife and gargantuan electricity bills. There's no better place to learn about stage illumination, and I spent a lot of my time designing complex lighting rigs for theatre and cabaret shows that went on to tour the world. After Vegas, designing light for gardens feels like child's play. The principles are exactly the same: I'm still lighting a subject, still concealing the light source and still controlling the size of the beam, it's just the 'stage' is a lot smaller and the 'stars' don't do much dancing!

Where budget allows, the lighting design is one of the more enjoyable aspects of my work.

It's also something I feel very strongly about. Without lighting, you're denying yourself the pleasure of your outdoor room at night and, for people with busy working lives, this is often their only opportunity to take advantage of the space during the week. One of the things I find myself saying to clients time and again is, you've paid for your domain, so why not ensure you can use it every hour of the day and night?

There's a magical quality to a well-lit garden. Light instantly transforms the space, highlighting features that are barely noticeable during the daylight hours and transforming the atmosphere with the flick of a switch, from soft and intimate to vivid and theatrical. This is a wonderful opportunity to let your imagination run wild.

BY DAY A MEDITATION pavilion partially screened by decorative awnings and engulfed in masses of varied foliage. At night, softly coloured lights create a scene of romance and mystery.

GETTING TECHNICAL

Don't baulk at the prospect of playing with lighting because it looks too technical. Believe me, the rudiments are easy to grasp and it can end up being one of the most fun, creative and satisfying aspects of planning and building your outdoor room. Here are some basic starting points for you to think about:

PLACEMENT My golden rule here is that the source should always be discreet. Don't get me wrong, there are some great-looking fittings around, but be careful they don't end up dominating – the focus should be on the garden and not the lighting fixture. Probably the most common lighting mistakes people make are to do with placing the light itself. For example, an up-light might be positioned too close to the subject, lighting only a small portion of it. And front-lighting the subject tends to wash out all of the subtle detail. If you light the same piece from the side, above or below, it suddenly comes to life and develops an interesting third dimension.

DIRECTION To maximise the architectural potential of a subject, think beyond the standard in-front lighting. Consider a side-casting light, drawing attention to a particular section of a wall or a hedge. This can look amazingly effective, throwing up wonderful shadowy shapes. Pillar lights that shoot a striking vertical beam are an excellent choice for an entrance or a wall, but be sure to place the light source at eye level, otherwise it will be uncomfortably dazzling for the observer.

'DIRECTIONAL LIGHT FROM HALOGEN GLOBES TURNS THE SCREENS INTO A MAGICAL BLUE, PURPLE AND DUSKY PINK BACKDROP, WHILE MOON–LIKE ORBS DRIFT ON THE SHIMMERING CORRIDOR OF WATER.'

INTENSITY This is all about the strength of the lights. You need to ensure the beam will travel far enough to light the subject in its entirety. In simple terms, we're talking wattage, so this factor will come into play when you're choosing your globes.

FOCUS I'm a big fan of low-voltage lighting because the globes come with a projecting angle of anywhere between 13 degrees (a directional pin-spot for small subject) and 65 degrees (to flood a hedge or tree). This gives you the opportunity to pour the focus on a particular object to the exclusion of all else. Great for the star features.

COLOUR Have you ever wondered why 24-hour convenience stores are awash with the bright white light of fluorescent bars? This is a deliberate ploy to deter 'undesirables' because stark illumination is not welcoming (some would say it's downright hostile). And how about the lights in dressing rooms? We've all experienced the harsh and unflattering effects of a white wash when we're trying

clothes on, whereas softer, warmer hues are far more forgiving and attractive. Well, the same principle goes for lighting your garden. This is why I tend to go for halogen globes or fibre-optic tubes which work well not just because of their low intensity and soft glow but also for the wonderful variety of shades they offer. If you decide to go for colour, the choice can be extremely important. Consider the mood you want to create and always remember that subtlety is the key. Too much variety can wind up looking tacky unless you are making a bold, contemporary statement and even then you have to be very sure of what you're doing. I've always favoured blue for its mysterious, underwater feel and warm, buttery yellows seem to go well anywhere. As a rule of thumb, try to choose colours that already occur naturally in your garden and complement these existing tones rather than using colours that contrast and undermine them. My best advice is to go for one, or maybe two basic tints, and follow a unifying theme throughout the space.

WHEN DARKNESS FALLS this rooftop really comes into its own, offering a great venue for parties. Light from the inside, enhanced by the reflection of a treacly timber floor, spills through cantilevered glass doors and louvre blinds. Rows of downlights take care of the immediate deck area, and directional spots shooting across tubs of wildly sprouting grasses set the mood for those wishing to have a quiet chat away from the centre of action. A borrowed lighting landscape is provided by city buildings twinkling merrily against the night sky several kilometres away.

THE LARGE-FORMAT timber platforms on this rooftop are sunk in a bed of washed pebbles that were created by tumbling rocks rather than mining river beds. Each pontoon is a different size to break up the rigid formal lines of the ground plane. Slatted timber screens inhibit strong gusts of wind while still revealing the city views in the distance. Baby Sun Rose (Aptenia cordifolia) tumbles from a row of window boxes (left).

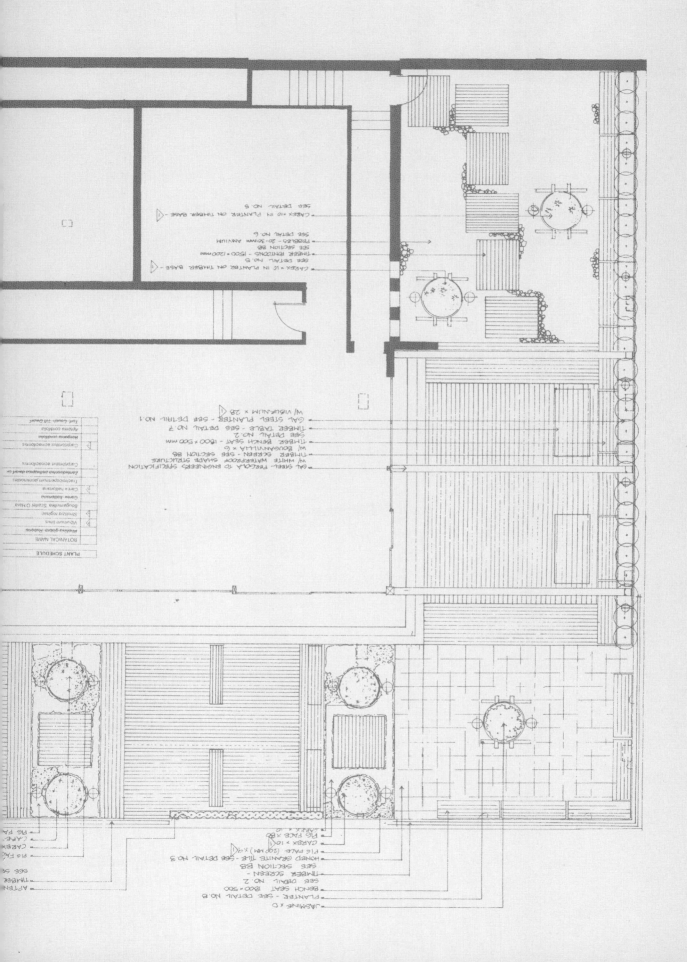

PLANT SCHEDULE

	BOTANICAL NAME
	Michelia yunnanensis
	Viburnum tinus
	Strelitzia reginae
	Bougainvillea 'Scarlet O'Hara'
	Carex halleriana
	Carex halleriana
	Trachelospermum jasminoides
	Lomandra longifolia 'Katrinus Deluxe'
	Carpobrotus acinaciformis
	Magnolia grandiflora
	Carpobrotus acinaciformis
	Agonis contorta
	Turf Couch 'Tall Green'

GAL STEEL PERGOLA to ENGINEERS SPECIFICATION
w/ WHITE WATERPROOF SHADE STRUCTURE
TIMBER SCREEN - SEE SECTION BB
w/ BOUGAINVILLA x 6
TIMBER BENCH SEAT - 1800 x 500 mm
SEE DETAIL NO. 2
TIMBER TABLE - SEE DETAIL NO. 7
GAL STEEL PLANTER - SEE DETAIL NO. 1
w/ VIBURNUM x 28

CAREX x 10 IN PLANTER ON TIMBER BASE -
SEE DETAIL NO. 5
TIMBER PARTITIONS - 1500 x 1200 mm
SEE DETAIL NO. 6
PEBBLES - 20-30 mm AMVIUM
SEE SECTION BB
CAREX x 10 IN PLANTER ON TIMBER BASE -
SEE DETAIL NO. 5

JASMINE x 6
PLANTER - SEE DETAIL NO. 8
BENCH SEAT 1800 x 500
SEE DETAIL NO. 2
TIMBER SCREEN -
SEE SECTION BB
HONED GRANITE TILE - SEE DETAIL NO. 3
PIG PALE (20 MM) x 40
CAREX x 10
PIG PALE x 80
CAREX A x 10
CARE
CAREX
APTEN
TIMBER S
SEE S
PIG PA

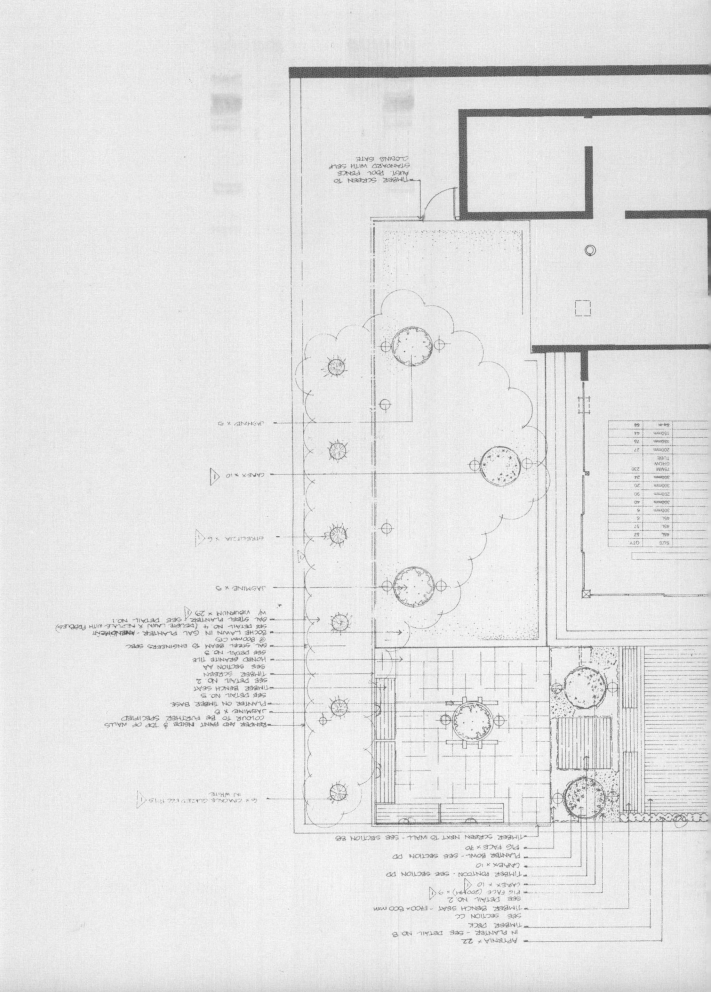

EDGY BUSINESS

When you start to draw up your lighting plan, it's important to consider the boundaries and access areas. Lighting the border of the space is necessary for security and for visual impact. Boundaries give the garden a sense of depth and scale. They provide standout features with a backdrop or emphasise their prominent position in the garden. A well-lit 'line' with darkness beyond creates a sense of intrigue and mystery – what's beyond the edge? – and the garden as a whole instantly gains a feeling of being enclosed within a shimmering frame. For access areas like a driveway or a pedestrian entrance, bollards are a good choice. When you position the lights on the perimeters, it's the spacings that make all the difference. Of course, much depends on the surrounding light situation (ie street lamps or spillage from nearby buildings), but your best bet is to space them anywhere between 1200mm and 2200mm apart. The rule here is, the darker the area, the shorter the intervals, and remember to clearly accent when the path turns or changes level. Don't make the mistake of placing up-lights in a position that will shine directly into the eyes. You'll notice that most bollard lights are placed so that they shine down onto the path for this very reason. Finally, entrance ways should always be a focus: a sort of 'announcement' of your property and a clear signpost so that it can be

ILLUMINATING THE WATER *that surrounds this courtyard accentuates the feeling that the floor itself is floating (left).* FROSTED GLASS *(centre) is an excellent material for reflecting and dispersing light. Add water to the equation for tremendous visual energy and drama.* BLENDING WITH THE *furniture theme, this bollard (right) has a chunky timber base and a cap of translucent resin that disperses an even glow.*

THE OVERWHELMING HEAT and dryness of Las Vegas is legendary, and these days many outdoor cafes in the desert city compensate with misting systems which shower a fine transparent rain on the patrons, cooling and re-hydrating them. This was the inspiration behind the rainforest seen here. It is canopied with a grid of creeper-clad hoses that spray a fine mist to constantly moisten and humidify the atmosphere. Flowing sheer fabric curtains envelope the space, shutting out the world from this tropical haven. And just like dry ice creeping across a stage, clouds of vapour look fantastic backlit by the setting sun.

easily found by first-time visitors. Maybe this is where you lash out and buy that special pair of lights you've been eyeing off so that the first sight of your home makes a bold statement about what lies within.

AC/DC

There are lots of choices out there, but I find that low-voltage lights are effective in most situations. You may pay a little more to start with but the effect is well worth it and you can feel good about the fact that they are safer than most other forms of lighting. You can easily lay a 12-volt cable yourself as long as you strictly follow the advice of the manufacturer or tradesman. Anything that involves 240 volts requires a professional to do the work.

On a personal level, I love the subtlety and versatility of fibre-optic lights but,

unfortunately, it's an expensive option (isn't that always the way?) and must be installed by a licensed tradesman. Fibre optics has been around for quite some time but only in recent years have its capabilities finally begun to be exploited in the garden. It comes in the form of a thin cable (like a garden hose) filled with thin translucent strands through which the light travels and is available in a variety of different sizes. The light moves through the fibres which can bend around corners, shoot a light from the cable end or emit a soft glow through the side of the cable for its entire length. One of the best things about it is you never have to change the lights in the cable and the only maintenance required is at the box where the light originates. Fibre-optic lights can withstand all sorts of weather conditions and they're famous for illuminating difficult areas like step treads and pool surrounds.

Another great feature is that you can purchase a rotating colour wheel which allows you to change the colour of the light according to the mood you want to achieve.

An important safety tip – and this is a biggie – make sure a cut-off switch is installed at every power source. You'd be surprised how easy it is to accidentally cut a cable in an outdoor space and the results, as you can well imagine, are far from pleasant.

BACKYARD MAESTRO

Now that the technical stuff is out of the way, it's time to let your imagination take over. Try to block all practical considerations from your mind and look at the garden in its purest form. I tend to design a lighting plan the same way I design a garden: focus on the shapes.

Begin by thinking of your outdoor room as a canvas that you are 'painting' with light. (It helps to think of the light as a tapered column of paint that starts as a slim, narrow beam and spreads into a radiant pool.) Now focus on the most prominent feature, whether it's a plant, sculpture or architectural detail, and carefully position the light for maximum effect. Determine from which angle the feature will be most frequently viewed and light that side, usually from the base to give the subject majesty and prestige. Work on highlighting the important details while throwing the shadowy depressions into sharp relief. This gives a wonderful sense of drama.

My advice is to first play around a bit with a torch, testing angles and potential shapes and shadows. Notice how a soft, well-placed light can lend glamour to even the most ordinary object. A good tip is that if the plants are in pots you can swap them around so different varieties of foliage can be moved into

DIRECTIONAL SPIKE LIGHTS smothered in lush groundcovers pick out the spongy tactile trunks and fronds of soft tree ferns.

BOLLARD LIGHT

STEPLIGHT

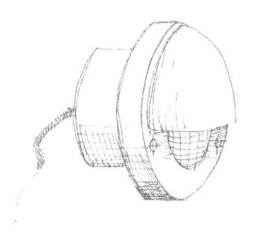

PILLAR LIGHT

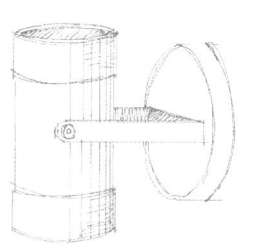

UPLIGHT

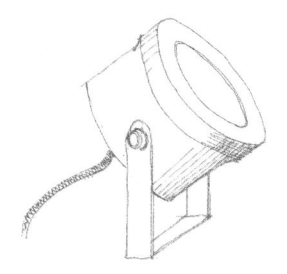

ADJUSTABLE SPIKE SPOT

the light and featured at the times of year when they look their best.

Trees can look especially breathtaking with the proper illumination. There is something so beautifully simple about the way light enlivens the architecture of the limbs and as it loses intensity passes on a subtle glow to the delicate foliage. For the grandest of statements, nothing looks more regal to me than an avenue of trees bathed in a rich golden glow.

As for feature plants, it's hard to make a bad choice: strong and simple to massed and feathery, they can all look fantastic when lit correctly. Dramatic, sculptural shrubs that lend themselves to lighting are *Acer palmatum* (Japanese Maple), all the magnolias, strelitzias and anything you find that has a unique shape with striking parallel lines or lateral branches. By day they blend in as an integral part of the green canvas, by night they become a stand-out feature that springs to life and takes on a whole new personality with the help of clever illumination.

SPIKY PLANTS OR *plants with simple form make a strong architectural statement when properly illuminated. Some great examples are these cycads (*Cycas revoluta, *right and* Encephalartos altenstenii, *left), cactus (centre left), Grass Tree (*Xanthorrhoea *spp., centre right) and Silver Fan Palm (overleaf).*

THE SPECIAL LIGHTING features in this garden mean it really comes into its own after dark. The passage of light itself is the focus of this stone pillar (left). The light is set within a 25mm recess that slowly tapers into flat stone, and the beam's intensity diminishes progressively as it travels down the carved corridor so that stone and light echo each other. Lit from below, the copper bowls in the water feature (below) appear to float above the smooth liquid surface, giving it an otherworldly feel. The water feature itself extends in steps down the side of the property, each spillway lit with a vertical strip to accentuate the movement of the water.

LIGHTING inspiration

filling a need

Australians have a deep passion for the great outdoors. Typically we are hardworking, and with the pressures and demands of life and the need to maintain our lifestyles we do tend to sacrifice our precious leisure time. We forget how important it is to have regular contact with the natural environment. I've been working since I was fifteen so I know what it's like trying to juggle the need for work, rest and play. I travelled the world for years in the entertainment industry, and a lot of that time was spent staring at hotel walls hankering for a sanctuary I could call my own: a peaceful place where I could simply relax and be myself. Somehow I've ended up in a career where I design exactly those kinds of spaces for other people, and even more ironic, now I have less down time than ever!

To compensate, I make sure I balance long days and working weekends with plenty of surfing and yoga, and I escape whenever I can to the beach or the bush for a bit of camping. Sometimes I find myself longing for a break, but like so many others who are building a career, that's just not always an option. So I sustain myself with the knowledge that a time will come when I can afford to take it easier and finally pour all my energies into creating my own retreat. I have to say, I daydream a lot.

There's an intriguing upside to the fact that I'm still hungry for my own place. Surrounded by the beautiful gardens I create every day, I automatically put myself in there, imagining what it would be like if it were mine. As a result, I've never designed a garden I wouldn't want to live with myself. My theory is that if I don't covet the place a little then I've not pushed the envelope far enough. Every time I finish a job, I want to walk away just a bit envious of the owners and at the same time proud to have designed the most attractive and useful space possible.

Acknowledgements

For those who don't know Geoffrey Bawa, to whom I have dedicated this book, he was born in Sri Lanka in 1919 and died in 2003. An ex-lawyer who took up architecture as a second career, he became one of the most prolific and influential architects of our time. He is most famous for creating intimate relationships between landscape and architecture and is one of the original composers of the 'outdoor room'. I had the pleasure of meeting Geoffrey Bawa and seeing his outstanding work firsthand in June 2002 at Lunanganga, his private estate in Sri Lanka. It was an experience I will never forget.

I never imagined I would have the opportunity to create another book, and although it's been extremely gratifying, no matter what anyone says, it doesn't get any easier the second time around. I could not have done it without the help of a very talented and special team.

Thank you to Sue Hines for listening to my dreams and making them a reality, to Rachel Lawson for your dedication, diplomacy and patience, to Jennifer Castles for your absolute poetry, to Briony Cameron for your commitment and humour, and to the rest of the dynamic team at Allen & Unwin. To Nick Mau, for laying out every page like a Picasso: thank you for graciously keeping in harmony with my vision. To Simon Kenny for making it all so easy: your beautiful photography is inspiring.

Thank you to the fantastic lecturers at Ryde Horticulture College, especially Janet Bate for your knowledge, support and genuine friendship. To David Gyngell, John Alexander, Michael Healey, Stuart Clark, Andrea Keir, Heidi Virtue, Julia Reynolds, Brendon Moo and the fantastic publicity machine at Channel 9. To my managers at IMG, in particular Chris Giannopoulos, Greg Hooton, Sean Anderson, Martin Jolly and Daniel Hill: you guys really are the dream-makers – thank you for your professionalism and support. To Don and Marea Burke and everyone at CTC Productions, including Ric Spence, Steve Macann and my beloved *Blitz*

team. And a special thank you to all the viewers who tune in each week and in particular to those who enjoyed my book last year. Without your support I would not be here. I hope you are inspired again this year.

On a personal note, thanks to Nadine Bush for your constant support and stylistic touch, and to Mum, Dad, Chris, Michelle, Taylor and the rest of my family and friends for your never-ending patience, loyalty and love.

I'm grateful to all of my clients for letting us back into their homes again, in particular the Koczanowski family. I hope we have shown your gardens in the best possible light. It has been a privilege to again be involved with the wonderful team at the Royal Botanic Gardens in Sydney. Thanks too to Planet Ark, especially Tanya Ha.

To my incredibly talented Patio team: Harriette Rowe for your patience, dedication, creativity and beautiful photographs, David Vago, Giselle Baron, Chuck Berry and Daniel Baffsky for your special contributions, Sebastian Tesoriero, Linda Cox and Nicola Starsmeare for your commitment and loyalty. This book is a testament to you all, it is an absolute pleasure working with a team I can laugh with – plenty more laughs on the way . . .

And finally, to Made Wijaya: your work is an inspiration to me and I cannot thank you enough for your kind words.

ROYAL
BOTANIC
GARDENS
SYDNEY

THE
FLORENCE
BAPTISTERY
DOORS

THE FLORENCE BAPTISTERY DOORS

PHOTOGRAPHS
DAVID FINN

INTRODUCTION
KENNETH CLARK

COMMENTARIES
BY GEORGE ROBINSON

THAMES AND HUDSON

FOR
HERBERT

Frontispiece: Joseph, from The Adoration of the Magi, North Door

Introduction © 1980 Kenneth Clark
Photographs © 1980 David Finn
Layout and commentaries © 1980 Thames and Hudson Ltd, London

Printed in Italy by Arnoldo Mondadori, Verona

CONTENTS

THE DOORS
OF THE BAPTISTERY
KENNETH CLARK

Almost the only complete works of art that have survived from the Middle Ages undamaged and unrestored are bronze doors. There are magnificent examples in the Low Countries and the Rhineland, e.g. Hildesheim, but the most numerous are in Italy. The bronze doors of the Baptistery in Pisa are amongst the first datable pieces of Italian sculpture; those of S. Zeno in Verona (*c.* 1150) show a knowledge of what used to be called 'the rules of art' much beyond any other sculpture of the mid-twelfth century. In parts of southern Italy where works of art are rare – Trani, for example – magnificent bronze doors have survived. In Tuscany there are bronze doors in Pisa, Lucca and Siena. But in the acknowledged centre of Italian art – Florence – the doors of the famous Baptistery were of wood, and those of the Cathedral were devoid of sculpture. One may imagine how much this situation distressed the city fathers, and in 1322 it was decided to commission doors for the Baptistery in which wooden reliefs were to be covered with gilt bronze. Apparently nothing came of this decision, which looks on the face of it a bad one, and in 1329 it was agreed that the doors should be of bronze. The guild responsible for the Baptistery, the Arte di Calimala, was instructed to send representatives to Pisa to study and make drawings of the bronze doors of the Cathedral, and then go to Venice, famous for its bronze casting, and see if there were craftsmen available to work on doors in Florence. Incidentally, it is remarkable that in a technical matter of this kind no progress seems to have been made since the doors of S. Zeno, cast almost three hundred years earlier. As so often, the fourteenth century proves to be a kind of recession from the triumphs of the high Middle Ages.

In 1330 comes our first reference to Andrea Pisano as *maestro delle porte*. He must have started work on the door some years previously, as by 2 April 1330 both leaves of the door were modelled in wax. By 1332 they were being cast by Venetian craftsmen, and the first was finished by the end of the year. As always, there was a long interval of chasing and polishing, and in 1336 the door was put in position. It was immediately acclaimed, and continued to be a source of pride to the Florentines long after the Quattrocento style had gone out of fashion.

After the success of Andrea Pisano's door it is surprising that the Florentine city fathers and the guild of the Calimala allowed over sixty years to pass before commissioning two more doors to accompany it on the Baptistery. But bronze doors are expensive, and the second half of the fourteenth century was a bad time for the Florentine economy. It was also a period of plague, and Florentine art in general was in recession. Thus at the turn of the century there was a revival of prosperity, and amongst the first signs of confidence was the famous competition for the Baptistery doors in 1401, in which seven sculptors were invited to submit trial pieces, the winner to be given the commission for all the remaining doors. Two of these trial pieces, those of Filippo Brunelleschi and Lorenzo Ghiberti, were considered much superior to the rest, and finally, says Ghiberti, 'The palm of victory was conceded to me by all the experts, as well as by all my fellow competitors.' He was therefore allotted the commission, although he was only twenty-two and no previous work of his is recorded. 'There were thirty-four judges,' says Ghiberti, 'some drawn from the city, some from neighbouring localities.' One must admire their courage, and marvel at their unanimity: indeed the whole story of the competition, read in comparison with any account of a similar episode today, makes one realize what confidence in the value of art existed in Florence in the early years of the fifteenth century.

The trial pieces (*Abraham and Isaac*) of Brunelleschi and Ghiberti still exist, and leave us in no doubt that the judges had made a good decision. The Brunelleschi is in some respects the more serious work, but its very sincerity has made it somewhat awkward and deprived it of rhythmic unity, whereas in the Ghiberti the whole episode is dominated by a flow of movement which even he never surpassed.

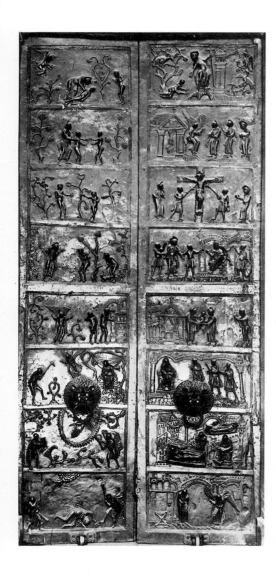

Bronze door of St Bernward
Hildesheim Cathedral, made in 1015

Bronze door of S. Zeno, Verona, *c.* 1150

Filippo Brunelleschi: bronze trial piece, showing *Abraham and Isaac*, made for the 1401 competition for the Baptistery doors (Bargello, Florence)

Lorenzo Ghiberti: *Abraham and Isaac*, the winning trial piece for the competition (Bargello, Florence)

The pattern which Ghiberti was ordered to follow was similar to that of Andrea's door, that is to say it was to be made up of twenty-eight panels, arranged in four columns of seven. The frames of each panel are powerful quatrefoils, and in many of them Ghiberti has taken full advantage of this form, using the pointed apex of the quatrefoil to clinch the presentation of the subject; for example, in the *Transfiguration* and *Resurrection* it becomes a sort of frame for Christ's head, and in the *Crucifixion* it gives special emphasis to the Cross. The scenes are amazingly various. Many of them are filled with figures in action – the *Expulsion of the Money-Changers*, the *Entry into Jerusalem*; but even in the most crowded, Ghiberti leads our eye to the figure of Christ. The sole exception is *Christ before Pilate*, where Ghiberti, with consummate art, makes the angry, vengeful priests the chief figures, while Christ, humble and resigned, stands behind the conformist civil servant, who washes his hands. It is a presentation of the scene curiously parallel to that of Rembrandt's etching. But the greatest of the scenes are quite simple, with the drama concentrated on one or two figures, as in the *Temptation*, the sublime *Crucifixion*, or the *Resurrection*. We feel that classic narrative art could not be carried further.

There is no evidence of the order in which the scenes were done. The biblical sequence does not help us, for the series begins at the third scene up in the left-hand tier, the *Annunciation*, which in its economy is like scenes in the upper registers, such as the *Flagellation*. Nor does Ghiberti attempt to relate the scenes to each other. Each one is a complete and self-sufficient image of the episode it portrays, and the longer one studies them, the more one is convinced by Ghiberti's intense seriousness. At first one is held prisoner by Ghiberti's style, but gradually one recognizes the *truth* of each scene, and realizes that it was this, above all, that mattered to the artist and his contemporaries.

Rembrandt: *Ecce Homo*, etching, 1655
(British Museum)

Ghiberti had relied heavily on the patience of his patrons. The work was said to be almost finished in 1417, but the doors were not put in place till 1424. The cost had been immense: 22,000 gold florins, which was as much as the annual defence budget of the Florentine Republic, while Ghiberti's salary was equal to that of a manager of a Medici bank. Nevertheless, as soon as the doors were completed the Calimala commissioned him to do another door, its subjects to be drawn from the Old Testament. Here the choice of subjects presented far more problems than the New Testament had done, and to allay controversy they were chosen by a humanist philosopher of unassailable learning and piety, Leonardo Bruni. There were originally to have been twenty narrative panels, but Ghiberti, who wished to do them on an expansive scale, cut down the number to ten, and in most cases put several incidents together on the same relief. There are as many as five on the *Cain and Abel* panel, and six on the *Noah*. It might be supposed that this would have meant the sacrifice of the concentration which is such a feature of the first series, but by this time Ghiberti had become such a master of composition that even the most complex scenes, like the *Joseph*, retain their unity.

230, 237

256

A few documents, chiefly payments to Ghiberti's son, give us dates for the progress of the work. By April 1436 ten narrative scenes and twenty sections of the surrounding pilaster had been cast, and were in the course of cleaning by Ghiberti, his son and assistants. By July 1439 the panels of *Cain and Abel* and *Isaac* were completed, but those representing the stories of Joseph and of Solomon were described as a quarter finished, which may well mean scarcely begun. The implication of this document is borne out by the reliefs themselves. The three upper panels on either side are faultless, in both design and execution. Ghiberti's desire to escape from the restricted quatrefoil of the earlier doors has taken almost palpable form. In the landscapes of *Genesis* and *Cain and Abel* we feel that we can move and breathe as in few other landscapes of the mid-Quattrocento. The architectural background of the *Isaac* panel is equally atmospheric. Unfortunately this feeling of space seems to have deserted Ghiberti about halfway through the project, and in three of the later panels, the *Moses*, the *Joshua* and the *David*, the figures are crowded together in confusing and featureless groups. Was this deterioration due, as is often claimed, to the use of assistants? Ghiberti had used assistants, including Donatello, on the first door. They were employed as executants, and I doubt if one of them would have been given a free hand to design important panels like the *Moses* and *Joshua*. We must accept the fact that

230

249

222, 230

263, 270, 277

by the time of the execution of the second door Ghiberti was over-extended. He was employed on various tasks in the Duomo, and undoubtedly designed several of the stained glass windows. So a greater use of assistants is not ruled out. But there was, I believe, a human reason why the later panels lack the inspiration of the first. The commission for the doors dragged on too long, and Ghiberti, who had his full share of Florentine restlessness, simply got bored with it. He produced work which could not be faulted, but was lacking in inspiration, However, in one of these late panels, probably the last of all, showing the meeting of Solomon and Sheba, he once more showed himself a master of spatial relationships. The architectural background is like an idealized picture of the Duomo with the façade removed. The groups to right and left of the central episode are amongst the first examples of that elaborate and calculated arrangement of figures that used to be thought of as one of the highest achievements of academic art. Critics have pointed out their affinity with

Leonardo da Vinci:
Adoration of the Kings,
1481 (Uffizi, Florence)

the *Adoration* of Leonardo da Vinci, perhaps because of the horses from Solomon's enormous stable that have broken in on the scene. But Leonardo's genius is so different that I would rather compare Ghiberti's *Solomon* with Raphael's *School of Athens*, where an equally elaborate composition embodies a similar feeling of a solemn occasion in which men have come together to witness the conjunction of wisdom and grace.

287

There are said to be almost a hundred figures in the panel of the meeting of Solomon and Sheba, and yet it makes no impression of over-crowding, only of harmony and decorum. 'It is arranged,' says Krautheimer, 'like the chorus in a Greek tragedy or, for that matter, a Verdi opera.' But Krautheimer's excellent comparison does, perhaps unwittingly, point to something that is unsympathetic to present-day taste: Ghiberti's unequalled skill in carrying a composition through to the last detail. To an age that so greatly admires *desinvoltura* – or 'sketchiness' – and an air of spontaneity, Ghiberti may seem to be too intent on perfection.

301–311

In the pilasters that surround the scenes of narrative are twenty full-length figures which include some of Ghiberti's most admirable inventions. A few of them can be identified as Old Testament characters – a handsome Jonah and an awe-inspiring Aaron; but the majority have no distinguishing marks, and they are usually described as prophets. One who can be identified without question is Samson, holding the jawbone of an ass, whose bearded head sits strangely on the beautiful body of an athlete. He is one of the most evolved nude figures of the Quattrocento, and was included simply in order that Ghiberti should display his knowledge of antique sculpture.

305

303

Raphael: *School of Athens*, 1509–11 (Stanza della Segnatura, the Vatican)

14

As in the North Door, the corners of the panels are marked by a series of heads, twenty-four in all. The majority of them are ideal heads, inhabitants of Ghiberti's imagination, who have insisted on being given visible form, and they are extraordinarily liberated from their epoch. Indeed, if some of them were removed and shown independently I doubt if many art historians could say where or when they were done. What a telling illustration of humanism that human heads should have taken the place of stylized plants as the motifs of decoration. As in the earlier door, Ghiberti has included his own head, and the contrast of this self-portrait with the likeness on the first door has become a commonplace of writings on the Quattrocento. It does indeed show very vividly the development from idealized trust to self-delighting realism. The serious young man, intently contemplating his visions, has become a wily old bird, accustomed to all the deceptions of the world, and remembering them half-humorously.

216

Finally, the outside frames of the doors contain an assortment of animals, birds and flowers, all observed with extraordinary accuracy. Although Ghiberti's figures are always outstandingly truthful, the realism of his observation of nature is a surprise. He must have studied Flemish manuscripts, and gained from them confidence to make his own observations as true to natural appearances as possible. The fusion of the naturalistic observation of a squirrel or a quail with formalized decorative motifs is an example of his skill as a designer; and once more we are struck by the influence of the doors on Raphael, who achieved a similar fusion in the decorations between the windows of the Loggetta in the Vatican. The likeness is too close to be accidental.

Ghiberti's second door does not 'date'. The tradition that Michelangelo called the two halves worthy to be the Gates of Paradise is proof of their fame in a period when most work of the mid-fifteenth century had gone out of fashion. Indeed we, who enjoy a 'period flavour', may think them almost too bland, and find more to our taste the Florentine accent of Donatello. This door is what Wölfflin defined as *klassische Kunst*. As with Raphael, we must overcome this prejudice and enter slowly into this timeless world, gratefully accepting a near perfect balance of ends and means, and of vision and design.

We shall be greatly helped in doing so by David Finn's magnificent photography. It is difficult to study, and still less easy to enjoy, the Baptistery doors *in situ*. The incessant traffic makes one nervous. At least half of each door, including the finest panels in the *Porta del Paradiso*, is too far up for one to see it in detail. I must have spent more hours than most in looking at the doors (partly because the tram to Settignano, where I lived, used to start from the Duomo), and I also had the good fortune to see them when they were being cleaned and the gold was miraculously re-appearing. But when I turn the pages of this enthralling volume I recognize how much I missed. Both Andrea Pisano and Ghiberti loved detail, and their panels contain significant and often surprising incidents that even David Finn admits he had not noticed until he was actually printing the photographs. I believe that there are details in this volume that will come as a surprise even to 'serious' students of the Quattrocento, and to the amateur they will have the effect of extending and humanizing his concept of Florentine art.

One of the many merits of David Finn's book is the prominence it gives to Andrea Pisano. He is one of those great artists who play little part in the history books, simply because we know practically nothing about him. Clearly he came from Pisa, but there is no evidence that he was related to Nicola or Giovanni Pisano, or that he had worked on the pulpit of the Cathedral. What had he done that the highly critical and slightly hostile Florentines should engage him to carry out one of their most important commissions? His style does nothing to help us answer the question. It is classical in its economy, and yet profoundly human. Inevitably he comes close to Giotto, with whom he worked in Padua. There is Giotto's concentration on the essence of each scene, and Giotto's humanity. But Andrea's feeling for human character is more diverse and subtly developed than that of Giotto. Giotto's men and women are types; Andrea's are individuals. There is a whole range of humanity among the subsidiary actors in each scene: look at the bearded man in the middle of the group 43 of believers who stand between Christ and John's disciples. He is absolutely true to life, and yet has a pathos which we associate with a later century. Through all this diversity, the Baptist remains a deeply human character, distinguished only by the authority of his inspiration. We feel it in his first appearance as a grown man and in his last, when his neck is bared to the executioner's axe. This head is almost without a trace of stylization. It is a piece of noble dramatic truth. Andrea's interest in humanity is particularly noticeable in the expressions on his faces, which go far beyond the more generalized types of Giotto. Where, for example, can one find in Giotto an observation as subtle as the expression of Zacharias when he learns that his aged wife shall, at last, conceive?

At least we can say that the quatrefoil panels in which the scenes are framed are Gothic, and a few of the heads show a memory of French fourteenth-century sculpture. But many of the heads that peer out from between their more stylized companions, as in plates 16 and 18, are completely dateless; they are Andrea's own personal discoveries, rediscovered by David Finn.

These discoveries become even more numerous when we come to the inexhaustible invention of Ghiberti. To name only a few in the North Door: the Satan recoiling from Christ's rebuff, and yet accepting it with a kind of wonder; the figure of Christ in the *Transfiguration* gravely aware of the   152 superhuman burden that his Father has placed upon him; and the head of Christ at the Last Supper which must surely be one of the noblest   161 representations of Our Lord in the whole of art. The minor figures are equally memorable, for example the boy on the ground in plate 140, and the head of the young man in the boat on the Lake of Genesareth. The   146 other passengers turn to him in alarm, but he is calm, because he has seen the figure of Christ walking on the water. It is proof of Ghiberti's mastery of narrative that the writer can scarcely restrain himself from describing these details. But the heads that he has placed at the intersections of the panels are almost equally riveting. I must mention three which are of particular interest: the dateless beauty in plate 187, the curiously 'modern' head of a woman in plate 186, and the head of a man in plate 189, which seems to be derived from an antique, perhaps a lost, bust of Caesar. Finally, he included a head of himself, which I have already described.

When he comes to the more familiar ground of the *Porta del Paradiso*, David Finn has been able to see afresh figures with which we are indeed well acquainted, but have never realized in their full sculptural existence. Such, for example, is Abel the little shepherd, who face is almost invisible   235 from a frontal view. In the *Noah*, how few of us have observed the pathos of   237 Shem's head as he turns away from the spectacle of his drunken father. It has an almost Michelangelesque nobility. I confess that I had never noticed the classical beauty of Esau's head as he barters his birthright with   253 his brother. In the later panels, so often lacking in a point of focus, but so admirable in detail, one finds the moving group of the elders carrying the   270 Ark; and the warring soldiers give us a new idea of Ghiberti's intention when he designed this confusing composition.

I have already mentioned details of the individual figures which are such a splendid feature of the volume. Ghiberti's range of sympathy is incredible, extending from the stern, commanding Aaron to the young prophet who has the delicate sensibility of a romantic poet. 'What an artist,' one murmurs, as one turns the last page; 'Why does he not occupy the same kind of position in the mind of the average art-lover as, say, Botticelli?' The answer is partly that his major work is all in one place. Theoretically it may be desirable for an artist to give the best of himself to a single great work, but from the point of view of his appeal to posterity, it is better that his works should be distributed, so that each may make a separate impact.

But there is another reason which is, perhaps, implicit in Krautheimer's excellent comparison of Ghiberti's great *scenas* with the choruses in a Verdi opera. There is in the masterly elaborations of these groups something alien to an age that admires *desinvoltura*, and distrusts completeness. We feel that such perfect unity can be achieved only by suppressing those individual characteristics which we discover with delight in the work of Donatello. David Finn's book shows us that this is an illusion. Ghiberti's characters are quite as individual as those of his great contemporary. The figures on the campanile are as full of inner life as those of Rembrandt; Donatello seems to have lived their lives. Ghiberti remains a spectator, but one whose marvellous powers of observation were never surpassed in the century after his time.

ON PHOTOGRAPHING THE BAPTISTERY DOORS

DAVID FINN

Some years ago, I photographed a number of details of the North Door of the Florence Baptistery for my own pleasure. I had seen many published photographs of its panels, but I wanted to explore for myself, through my camera lens, some of the individual figures and faces which were so finely designed and executed. My hope was to create photographs which would be as powerful in themselves as the remarkable forms my eye saw when looking closely at the details of the sculptures. At that time I photographed only a few figures at eye-level. Because of the heavy iron railing in front of the door, however, I was not able to get as close to the figures as I wanted, and the 35mm camera I used proved inadequate for what I wanted to accomplish. The prints I made were dull and clumsy, and had none of the sharpness or brilliance of the originals. Since the eye-level panels of the East Door – the 'Gates of Paradise' – were so complicated I made no attempt to photograph any of their details. I felt that it would be impossible to focus my camera on individual figures in those scenes, to say nothing of the higher ones, with the equipment I had. Besides, the iron railing and the constant crowds in front of that door made me think that anything more serious than snapshots was not possible. (I doubt whether anyone visiting Florence with a camera in recent years has *not* photographed the East Door; it must be one of the most photographed objects in the world.) Nor did I, at the time, think of photographing the

South Door. Indeed, the fame of the Ghiberti doors so overshadowed the Andrea Pisano door for me that I hardly took the time to look at it carefully.

A few years later, I made a second attempt, this one more ambitious because I included all three doors, used a Hasselblad camera and photographed as many details as I could. I was still working just for my own pleasure, but when I printed these photographs from the larger format 2¼-inch (120-mm) square negatives, the results were far more promising, and I began to formulate the exciting plan of photographing details of what might be collectively one of the most beautiful examples of relief sculptures in the world. The notion of doing a book developed when I showed some of my early prints to Eva Neurath of Thames and Hudson, who encouraged me to follow through with my idea.

With the help of local authorities during several visits to Florence, I had the benefit of ladders to get close-up photographs of all the panels at all levels. I had to use a 20-foot (6-metre) extension ladder which was tall enough to rest on the wall of the building just above the door (the doors are a little over 16 feet, about 5 metres, high), as well as a free-standing ladder that could be placed close to the doors. Some of the photographs were taken only inches away from the figures, with close-up lenses, and often I had to stretch far out from the top of the long ladder, balancing myself precariously with the camera in one hand and holding on to the ladder with the other, confident that I was risking my life for a worthy cause.

As I set to work on Andrea Pisano's South Door, it was a revelation to me, especially when I photographed details of its upper panels. The lower figures of the virtues, which are what most of us see if we look at the door at all, had always been striking but archaic to me, and I had never had the opportunity to look closely at the dramatic figures above. While I was photographing these upper panel figures, I realized how successful a fusion they are of the great strength of late medieval sculpture and the emerging sophistication of the early Renaissance. Ghiberti must have felt challenged even to match the quality of these sculptures.

The North Door was more difficult to photograph than the South and the East Doors, for the light falling on it is considerably poorer. Even on bright days the figures are in the shade, and I had to take many chances on slow-speed exposures. But the superb realism of Ghiberti's figures was a constant fascination as I moved from panel to panel: again and again, I discovered details I had not known existed, even though I had examined the panels many times from the street level. One surprise, for instance, was

to discover the beautifully modelled faces in the *Last Supper* that are turned 162
in to the door, and which a viewer cannot see from the street. I had never
before noticed such details as the man with the monkey in the *Adoration of* 125
the Magi, or the moving Leonardo-like faces in the *Entry into Jerusalem*, or 159
the beautiful details of the lamps and desks, and the pens, inkwells and 87–111
calligraphy in the books of the Evangelists and Church Fathers in the
panels at the bottom of the door.

Curiously, I expected a letdown when I started photographing the East
Door. Initially, I thought the reliefs would have less sculptural value
because of Ghiberti's obvious showmanship in these later works, and I was
afraid that photographs of the details would reveal this most famous of the
doors to be the least successful artistically. My fears were groundless, however. Beginning with the four renditions of Adam and the three of Eve in 222
the first panel and ending with the milling crowds in the depiction of the 287
meeting of Solomon and Sheba in the last, the figures show no falling-off of
the sculptor's sincerity and dedication. The finished quality of the scenes,
and the intricate but remarkably realistic three-dimensional effect, as in
the architectural renderings in the *Isaac, Joseph, Joshua, David* and *Solomon* 249, 256, 270,
panels, create a majestic setting for the great variety of dramatic figures. 277, 287
The work is more sophisticated, with techniques ranging from flat relief to
free-standing figures, but its inner strength is on a par with the sculpture of
the other doors. The four panels at eye-level of the East Door – *Moses,* 263
Joshua, Isaac and *Joseph* (these are the second and third rows from the 270, 249, 256
bottom) – are looked at most carefully by passers-by, and they are
exceptionally intricate. The *David* and *Solomon* panels, at the bottom of the
door, are equally complicated, and visitors find it even harder to 'read'
these because of the protective glass panel which has been placed in front of
them, and because the scenes are more highly populated. But I had no
difficulty discovering many fine details in them with my camera, especially
after workmen removed the glass panel and lowered the iron railing to a
position below the sidewalk. Angular views were especially revealing in
this door, too. As on the North Door, there are a number of faces not visible
from the street which proved to be quite lovely when my camera explored
them from different angles. A striking example is in the scene of Adam and
Eve being expelled from the Garden in the *Genesis* panel, where Adam, 222
hiding behind Eve, is almost invisible from the ground; only at the level of
the panel is it possible to see what is actually going on.

It took me many months to print my more than a thousand photographs
(only a portion of which have been included in this book), but the

developing and printing process was just as rewarding a part of the experience as taking the photographs. There were many details I had missed even when looking through my viewfinder, and I was delighted to see them appear in my developing tray. Perhaps most exciting in the East Door were the details of the faint relief of Eve plucking the apple for Adam, the sheep scratching its ear while Abel and a shepherd dog sit watchfully near by, the rhythmic movement in the figures of Noah's family, the Jerusalem cityscape in the *David* panel and the three figures carrying grain in the *Joseph* panel, which in their present state have a Rembrandt-like appearance.

227
235
240
284, 286
262

In the photographs of the North Door, I was impressed by Ghiberti's mastery of textures: the flowing robes in so many figures, particularly the Mary in the *Annunciation* where one can almost feel the body beneath the clothing, the texture of the ship's mast, sails and ropes in *Christ walks upon the Water* and the stubble on the shaven chin of Ghiberti's early self-portrait. The heads and figures of both Ghiberti doors, so many of them startlingly lifelike as portraits, are magnificent. The prints of some of the portraits, four or five times actual size, show how well they hold their form and how powerful the images remain when enlarged.

117
143

On Andrea Pisano's door, I was deeply moved by the noble face of Zacharias, the beauty of Herod's wife, the grief-stricken expression of those attending the burial of St John, the wonderful birds in the baptism of Christ, the two faces of the single figure of Prudence and the striking lion motif on the door's borders, in which Andrea Pisano displayed a remarkable knowledge of animal emotions.

10, 57
59, 27
74, 75, 76
77

While I was making my prints of the Ghiberti doors, I compared the results with those that have appeared in previous books, and I remembered Professor Krautheimer's warning to me, when I first told him about my project, that the panels had not been cleaned for a number of years. As it turned out, this was not a problem for me. If one wants to document the works for art-historical or archival purposes, then, of course, cleaning is essential, as are a scaffold, lights, a tripod, and a large-format camera. But this had been done quite adequately before, and it was not at all my objective. I wanted to rediscover in all three doors what the sculptors themselves had seen as they worked on the many different details of their figures. I wanted to follow their eye, as they used their modelling tools to bring one or another aspect of the sculpture up to their standards of perfection – seeing the figures not only straight on from the front, but from above, from behind, from the side. Perhaps most of all, I wanted to create photographs which I hoped the sculptors themselves would have enjoyed seeing, because they were photographs which captured the spirit of their work rather than merely recorded a single, technically accurate picture of the sculptural topography.

I felt that this spirit or character of the three doors was not at all affected by the changes wrought by the atmosphere; indeed, to my eye the residue of years of weathering has produced a quality in the sculptures which is extraordinarily touching. Often I was astonished by the richness of the graphic qualities which emerged as I worked on the prints: the beautifully composed combinations of blacks, greys, whites; the contrasts of delicate lines and solid tones; the expressiveness of figures that looked as if they had been boldly sketched in charcoal or etched brilliantly on a copper plate. These were not my achievements as a photographer: I (and my camera) succeeded in discovering and presenting in photographic prints the qualities that Andrea and Ghiberti had created with what seems an uncanny anticipation of how time would affect their works. Some of the photographic images, such as Andrea's face of the baptized Christ, 30 Ghiberti's portrayal of Joseph peering from behind a column in the 114 *Adoration*, and the figure of the drowned man in the *Noah* panel, look as if 245 they could have been created as graphic counterparts to the three-dimensional works, with the encrustations of weathered bronze creating dramatic textures which heighten the emotional powers of the scene. In some instances I have deliberately chosen a print which is less literal than others, because I find it more expressive of the experience of actually *looking* at the sculpture. Thus, for the picture of Eve rising out of Adam's 226 rib, I discarded a photograph taken in the sunlight, which revealed the full three-dimensional body of the figure and the faces of the angels around her, in favour of a more subtle and sensitive detail taken in the shade, whose effect is of a delicate line-drawing, beautifully expressing the mood of Eve's creation.

The colour photographs presented their own special difficulties. I used a rather slow film (64 ASA), which meant that I had to open my shutter wide, thereby reducing the depth of field and narrowing the segment of the sculpture which would be in focus. On the North Door, which is always in the shade, I also had to experiment with such slow speeds as 1/15 and 1/8 second, and this is extremely risky for hand-held shots. So it was especially gratifying that so many transparencies revealed the full majesty of the figures with their magnificent patination. The creativity in shooting colour – at least for me – was in the act of photographing rather than in the darkroom, but the results were often breathtaking. Thus, for instance, I

217, 218 think the colour plates of the reclining figures of Noah and his wife are little
8 jewels; the photograph of the sword-wielding executioner on the South
Door is especially powerful when one can see the colour of its patina; the
85 sleeping figure in the *Resurrection* on the North Door is beautiful in its
216 golden magnificence; and, of course, the self-portrait of Ghiberti on the
East Door is a masterpiece comparable to Rembrandt's great self-portraits.
Although the black-and-white photographs are more personal statements
from my point of view as a photographer, I believe that the remarkable
quality of the weathered gold patina of the figures can be most fully
appreciated in the rich colour prints.

When I finished my work, from photographing to printing, I felt that I
had become part of the doors, as if, through my photographs, I had joined
the sculptors in making a creative contribution to their work. The
experience was similar to memorizing a poem, when the words become
almost as much one's own as the poet's. So familiar was I with the
sculptures that I even wondered if I would ever be able to look at the
originals again with a fresh eye. 'Only that which is completed can be
known and dismissed,' wrote Yeats; having completed my photographs,
would I now dismiss the doors as things which I knew in their entirety?

Not long after I delivered my photographs to the publisher, I visited
Florence and walked somewhat apprehensively to the Baptistery. For the
first time in years I didn't have my camera with me, and I thought I would
feel a letdown without the excitement of searching for new ways of looking
at the sculpture, new details to discover, new views to relish. My worries
proved to be unwarranted. The opportunity for new adventures was as
great as ever. I had not exhausted my sense of discovery after all. If I had
had my camera with me then I would have gone on and on for hours. And
I'm sure I will feel the same whenever I visit the Baptistery in the future,
with my inner eye snapping the shutter, fixing in my brain, if not on my
photographic paper, new combinations of forms, textures, faces and figures
in those remarkable works which have enriched my life so greatly.

THE SOUTH DOOR

ANDREA PISANO

1

THE SOUTH DOOR

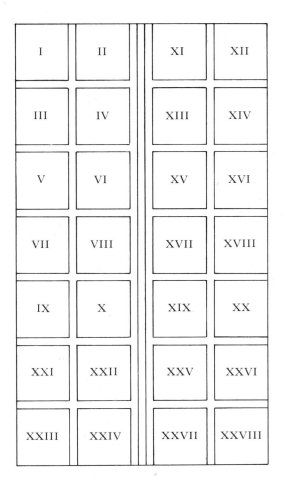

I	II	XI	XII
III	IV	XIII	XIV
V	VI	XV	XVI
VII	VIII	XVII	XVIII
IX	X	XIX	XX
XXI	XXII	XXV	XXVI
XXIII	XXIV	XXVII	XXVIII

Inevitably, perhaps, when it was decided in 1322 that an artist should be commissioned for the creation of a door at the east side of the Baptistery of Florence, the theme prescribed was the life of John the Baptist, eponymous patron of all baptisteries and prime analogue of their special function. Precedents for the theme existed in Italy before Andrea Pisano began his work: frescoes in the baptistery at Parma, the architraves of the main portals of the baptisteries in Pisa (Andrea's native city) and Parma, and various fonts, altar frontals and pulpits elsewhere. Indeed, a pulpit showing the story of John the Baptist had been commissioned for the Florence Baptistery in 1321 and was completed about two years after Andrea's door was hung, though it no longer survives.

Within the Baptistery itself, the mosaics in the dome constitute the most extensive illustration of the life of the Baptist done before Andrea Pisano set to work.

Altogether, then, the commission to Andrea, and later to Ghiberti, was a token of the pride and ambition the people of Florence felt for their Baptistery and their determination that it should be recognized as outstanding among all the baptisteries in Italy. Dante, that quintessential but exiled Florentine, remembers the Baptistery and calls it his 'bel San Giovanni'.

We know from documents that Andrea Pisano's door, hung in 1336, originally occupied the position of honour on the east side of the Baptistery, facing the Cathedral. On certain great liturgical occasions the doors of both buildings were opened, and a procession of catechumens passed from the Cathedral into San Giovanni for baptism. Andrea's door was eventually moved, some ninety years later, to make way for Ghiberti's first door, and was set up on the south, in the entrance still commonly used today.

Andrea Pisano himself is a somewhat hazy figure. He came from Pisa, and according to Vasari was first called to Florence to work on the west front of the Cathedral, designed by his close friend Giotto. (Later he was to be in charge of architectural work on the Cathedral.) When he received the commission for the door he was considered 'the most talented, skilful and judicious master ... in all Italy'. In conclusion, Vasari reminds his own contemporaries that Andrea 'merits the highest praise' – for 'what is beautiful, difficult and good' in Ghiberti's doors could never have been achieved without the example of the earlier sculptor's work.

And what a work it is! Cast in bronze, the two leaves of the door are divided each into two vertical columns of seven panels. The two lower horizontal rows depict eight virtues: Hope (*Spes*), Faith (*Fides*), Charity (*Charitas*), Humility (*Humilitas*), Fortitude (*Fortitudo*), Temperance (*Temperantia*), Justice (*Iustitia*) and Prudence (*Prudentia*). These are at the lowest level – less easily seen, perhaps, because of the door's height and certainly less important to be seen than its principal theme – and are both literally and figuratively the basis on which the Baptist's life rests.

The upper parts of each leaf of the door are to be read as one reads a book: left to right, top to bottom. Andrea combines all the Gospel stories mentioning John, and has created out of them a visual epic, in which from the very beginning the hero strives to reach his goal, suffers an ordeal and triumphs in the paradox of his own death. In this approach, Andrea was sensitively faithful to John's own claim that his was merely a 'voice crying in the wilderness': he was the Precursor, his life and death something of a 'rehearsal' for Christ's.

With this same sensitivity, Andrea generates a narrative tension from beginning to end of his story by paradoxically naive details. The literally dumbfounded Zacharias, for example, is obviously an old man who accepts on faith and with hope (the supporting virtues to the first two columns of the door) the angel's announcement that his old and barren wife Elizabeth is pregnant. In the *Visitation* panel, Mary already has a halo, as the mother of the Messiah. Much later, in the right-hand leaf, the court of Herod looks more like the setting for a masque than the place described by the Gospels and historians as teeming with incest, sensuality and betrayal. Andrea's Salome is rather a precocious but demure teenager than a seductive step-daughter manipulating Herod's desire; and when John's head is brought to Herod, who gestures that it is to be given to Salome, she folds her arms across her breast in a gesture of helpless confusion, as though realizing at last that she has been a pawn in the conflicts of adults. Finally, in his last two scenes, Andrea Pisano recalls and strengthens the analogy of John's life to Christ's. Using conventional 'deposition' and 'burial' motifs, he shows John's body being carried from prison (we are to 'forget' that John was decapitated and that this management of his body would, therefore, be awkward if not impossible) and his burial, in what looks very like a monastic setting with, even, an attendant acolyte standing by.

Through all the panels, Andrea contrives to sustain narrative progress, so that each incident implies the consequences appearing in its successor. By the end, we have witnessed and been moved by a story whose tragedy was contained in its beginning and which needed the subtle and allusive genius of Andrea Pisano to tell without artificial grandiosity.

The captions to colour plates 2–9 are on page 37.

4

5

7

9

PANEL I

10

The Angel and Zacharias: The father of John the Baptist, who was called Zacharias, was a high priest. According to ancient custom, the high priests took it in turns to carry out the various requisites of ritual in the Temple. Andrea Pisano, following the account given by Luke in his Gospel, here presents Zacharias swinging the censer containing the smoking incense it was his obligation to burn in the sanctuary, and wearing the bell-fringed garments and mitre-like headdress prescribed by the Law. As Zacharias stood at the altar, a place whose holiness was indicated by the lamps burning above it, an angel appeared to him. Reassuring the old man in his understandable fear, the angel, who said his name was Gabriel, told Zacharias that his prayer for a child at last had been heard: his wife Elizabeth would bear a son, who must be named John, that is 'Yahweh is Gracious.' Zacharias objected that he and his wife were already getting on in years, and that he needed a sign that what Gabriel had told him was true. In a tone of admonition, whose gesture Andrea has caught here, Gabriel declares that he stands in God's presence; because of Zacharias' weakness of faith, he will be speechless until the message brought to him has been fulfilled. Andrea's arrangement of the confronting figures, both taut but calm in the high importance of their encounter, conveys the intimacy of this strange meeting. Where they stand is ordinarily a place of ritual silence and belief: for his slowness of belief, Zacharias will be speechless until the fulfilment of Gabriel's message.

Detail: 14 angel

PANEL III

12

The Visitation: Zacharias, after his time of service in the Temple had been completed, returned home, and some time later his wife Elizabeth became pregnant. At last, Luke reports her saying, the Lord had pitied her and removed the stigma of barrenness. She withdrew from society for five months, but in her sixth month was visited by her young kinswoman, Mary, who had herself been visited by the angel Gabriel. In Mary's case, Gabriel's message was of tremendous import: she would miraculously conceive, and bear, the Messiah. As though to prove the truth of his announcement to Mary, Gabriel added the news that her cousin Elizabeth, whom everyone had considered barren, was already in the sixth month of her pregnancy. Mary, who is here accompanied by another young woman, perhaps a servant but certainly the companion convention would have demanded for such a journey, went as quickly as she could to her cousin in Ain Karim, a village not far from Jerusalem. On her arrival, as she called out to greet Elizabeth, the unborn John the Baptist leapt in his mother's womb, a movement Elizabeth understood as his recognition of the One whom Mary carried. The old woman's inspired intuition and the gentle candour of Mary are caught in this group by Andrea Pisano, who has exquisitely conveyed the inevitable clumsiness of the aged Elizabeth's pregnancy.

Detail: 15 Mary's companion

PANEL II

Zacharias is struck dumb: While Zacharias and Gabriel were within the sanctuary of the Temple, the people of the congregation wondered why the priest was so long about his duties. At last, he came out from the sanctuary. To everyone's consternation, however, he could not speak. It is that moment that Andrea reproduces here, with Zacharias pointing to his mouth in a gesture of mutism, while his left hand is poised in the embarrassment of confusion and wonder. Though he has left the inner sanctuary, his carriage and expression are of a man who has not yet regained his composure after a shocking experience. The onlookers, too, most of them of his own age and thus likely to have had their own anxieties about what may have happened to keep him so long at his duties, gesture in what Andrea succeeds in conveying as confusion and wonder. Luke tells us that they understood Zacharias had had a vision, and the figure in the middle of the panel points upwards, in a traditional gesture of prophecy, as though to indicate the source of Zacharias' puzzling condition. His neighbour seems lost in his own thoughts, perhaps wondering about the meaning of what has happened and, more important, its consequences.

Detail: 16 onlookers

PANEL IV

The Birth of John the Baptist: At length, the time for Elizabeth's confinement arrived and, just as Gabriel had told Zacharias, she bore a son. Because of her social position as a priest's wife, and probably also because her advanced age for childbirth had stimulated her neighbours' concern, Elizabeth's safe delivery was an occasion of joy in Ain Karim. Greater than either of these reasons, however, was the fact that her long barrenness had at last been fulfilled not merely by a pregnancy but by the birth of a son. Luke reports that her neighbours shared her joy at such a blessing from the Lord. In this panel, the sculptor makes Elizabeth concentrate her gaze and all of her attention on her child – quite large for a newborn! – who is being bathed and clothed by two seated attendants, perhaps midwives. Although they have come as visitors, and are bearing gifts of food (a conventional symbol of a confinement) whose containers' number and shape will later be echoed by Ghiberti's Magi (plate 114), the two women behind Elizabeth, obviously her neighbours, have not yet got her attention; one of them is about to remove the lid from the container she holds, as though hoping that at last her wish to contribute to Elizabeth's happiness will be acknowledged.

Details: 17 neighbour; 18 Elizabeth

15

PANEL V

The Naming of John the Baptist: Eight days after his birth, custom prescribed that the infant son of Zacharias and Elizabeth be circumcised and named. According to Luke's Gospel, when the moment came for his naming, it was assumed by friends and relatives that the boy would be called after his father. Elizabeth, however, who had obviously been told by her husband about the visit from Gabriel, said that he should be called John. As there was no one of that name in the family of either parent, the final decision was left to the still mute Zacharias, who took up a tablet and wrote on it, 'His name is John.' In all these respects, Andrea's panel of John's naming remains true, at least by implication, to the Gospel narrative.

Luke, however, explicitly states that Mary had returned to her own home before John's birth (though it would more probably have been the case that she would remain with her aged cousin to attend her in her confinement), and Andrea's justification for including her here, holding the child, may have come from the *Golden Legend*, a collection of lives of the saints and their legends, which was written about 1275, not long before work started on the door. According to it, Mary 'carried out the task of receiving John the Baptist at his birth' and of presenting him for naming. With a touching delicacy, the sculptor reminds us that Zacharias' vision, though it occurred during his function as a priest, was directly concerned with his ordinary life: he is shown here without priestly garments or apparel, a mute old man who must write what he is unable to speak.

PANEL VI

John goes into the Wilderness: All four Evangelists refer to the young John's leaving his home to live in the wilderness, a retreat from society that in every culture is associated with the prophet's or holy man's preparation for his life-mission. John's garments, we are told, were camel-hair and skin and, according to Matthew, a leather belt. Andrea portrays him so clothed here, adding according to convention a staff topped with a cross-bar, which forecasts the cross of Christ, whom John will later proclaim. Despite his youth, John is determined, undaunted by the austerity and harshness of 'the wilderness'. The trees Andrea Pisano has introduced would be surprising in a desert wilderness were they not perhaps locust trees, whose seed-pods (still, in some places, called 'St John's Bread') were, according to the Gospels, John's food, along with honey. Equally remarkable in this panel, if only for their size and number, are the birds which Andrea has included. When Elijah, that prophet of the old dispensation, was sent by Yahweh into the desert east of Jordan, he was fed by ravens. Andrea may have thought to recall by including these large birds that John's going into the wilderness was in order to prepare himself to be Precursor, or a prophet like Elijah, a comparison Christ will later make. The small lizard at the far right, scurrying off as John advances, will figure in the next panel as well.

Details: 21 John; 22 bird on a rock; 23 bird in a tree

19

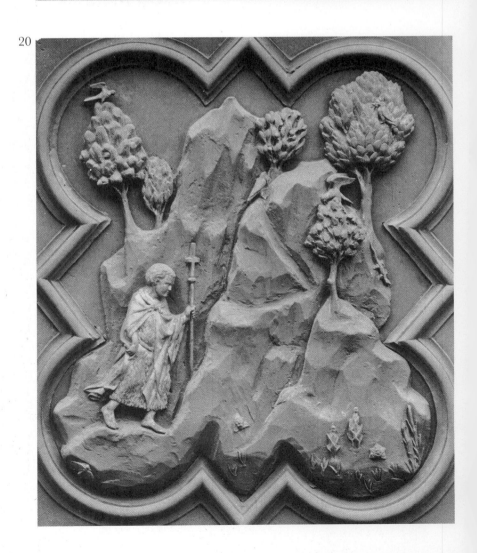

20

PANEL VII

John preaches to the People: John the Baptist's first appearance out of 'the wilderness' was to preach a general baptism as a token of repentance and of a turning back to God. Here Andrea presents John coming back onto the scene of the every-day world, his garments the rough coat of camel's skin that Matthew describes, and his hair unkempt and wild. Not yet the 'Baptist', he stands still tentative, as though the sculptor wanted the viewer to understand and to feel for himself what it means to be a 'Precursor', crying in the wilderness: 'make straight the way of the Lord'. John's audience here, who may be Pharisees, those rigidly legalist sectaries who would have reacted to John's appearance, behaviour and attitude as radical and shocking, remain aloof, calculating, unmoved. The one man whose face looks squarely out of the panel draws us into it and involves us in the drama of John's life, which here begins its public phase. And what of the small reptile scurrying down and away – one of the 'viper's brood', as John described the Pharisees, suspicious of their opportunism in coming to him for baptism?

Detail: 28 John preaching

PANEL IX

John baptizes the People: No longer Precursor, John now becomes the Baptist, administering that baptism by water, which he has identified as peculiarly his own, to his disciples. John's baptism, which Andrea here has him administering with a ritualistic detachment, is initiatory: it prepares a body of believers for their eventual reception into the company of Christ's disciples. It is a commitment, primarily to John but ultimately to Christ, and the subsidiary figures in this panel are no longer onlookers or audience. They are drawn by tension to the point of participating in the activity. Andrea has modelled them with such sensitivity that they appear to be huddled more closely together than in the two preceding panels, as though struck, at last, by the significance of what they are witnessing. John's initiation is a token, and by water; the baptism he has said that Christ will bring will be by the Spirit, and of fire. Now that John has proclaimed that difference, and begun his own ministry, his own fate must soon be made clear and lived out.

25 **PANEL VIII**

Behold the Lamb: Already John has authority, presence. As he defines his role as the harbinger of Christ, he appears established in that function. Andrea centres him in this panel, making him the link between Israel and Christ, whose future cross already tops John's staff and who stands by and above, waiting himself for the baptism it is John's mission to administer. John holds a scroll inscribed 'Ecce Agnus' (Behold the Lamb), proclaiming Christ as the sacrificial Lamb of God. The onlookers here are no longer mere interested spectators: Andrea draws them into the scene, as they follow John's pointing hand to look past him at a columnar Christ, whose own gaze looks beyond them into the future. This, says John, is the one who has come who is mightier than I; he will baptize not with water, as I do, but with the Spirit, and with fire. He will sift you like grain and throw the chaff on the fire he has prepared, a fire that will never be quenched. As a counterpoint to this awesomeness, the landscape here is rocky but full of the promise of change. The desert barrenness of John's first appearance, with its stunted shrub and scaly reptile, has given way to a world where flowers blossom, and trees may spread their branches in hope and growth.
Detail: 29 Christ

27 **PANEL X**

John baptizes Christ: Now, at last, comes the event that is both the acme and turning-point of John's life: he baptizes Christ in the River Jordan. The sculptor appears to emphasize this crucial importance of John's function by focusing imaginative attention on John's hand, poised above Christ's head as the baptismal water flows from the bowl it holds. Equally, in representing the dove, which Matthew and John say was the Holy Spirit, and by adding an attendant angel, the only personage not specified in the Gospel narrative, Andrea interrupts briefly the sequence of his door's panels as chronicle: this is not an episode of earthly history so much as part of eternity's unfolding its plan for men. The moment here is that of the first manifestation of the Trinity: Christ the Incarnate Son is hovered over by the dove of the Spirit while, Matthew tells us, a voice from heaven is heard saying, 'This is my beloved son, in whom I am well pleased.' This panel comes numerically at the end of the first half of John's story; in this event he is both Precursor, in acknowledging Christ and his relation to the Father and the Spirit, and Baptist, the human instrument through whom Christ will henceforth assume his mission among men.
Details: 30 Christ baptized; 31 John

28

30

PANEL XI

John before Herod: It had been laid down in Leviticus that a man must not have intercourse with, much less pretend to marry, his brother's wife. When, therefore, Herod the Tetrarch – or governor – of Galilee had John arrested and brought to him, he must obviously have been trying to brazen out his irregular domestic situation before John, who had after all by this time gained the reputation for urging all people to repentance. For Herod, called Antipas and son of that Herod the Great who had years before ordered the Slaughter of the Innocents, was living as though in marriage with Herodias, who had been his brother Philip's wife. John, despite his holiness, cannot be credited with tact, and he faced the Tetrarch with his crime and sin: 'It is unlawful for you to have your brother's wife.' Herodias, Mark says, was furious and wanted John killed, but Herod respected John's holiness and was in awe of him for his influence with the people.

With outstanding economy, Andrea reproduces the encounter here, charging each of the figures with a particular and appropriate emotion conveyed by stance and gesture. The forthright and impetuous John, though a prisoner, raises his hand towards Herod as though to remind him that *he* is the guilty one; Herod sits rigidly, perhaps astonished that not even the dignity of his position can any longer defend him from his guilt. Herodias draws back in repugnant fury, her hands raised and held in a position of frustrated rage. The attendant guard has an expression of waiting speculation.

Detail: 36 John accusing Herod

32

PANEL XII

John is imprisoned: Herod's pretext – he could not have justified his action on the basis of John's accusation – for imprisoning the Baptist was that he was a disturber of the peace and of good order. On the other hand, Herod would not, or could not yet, have John executed for fear of the reaction of the people, who loved him and followed him as a prophet. Out of this quandary, Herod took the way of the time-server: he had John thrown into prison, without having decided yet what to do with or about him. And this, Luke says, merely added to all the other evil things Herod had done. Striking in the panel is the contrast between the three guards accompanying John to his cell and the Baptist's attitude. He seems to be rushing forward into confinement, eager to fulfil his fate and destiny. The guard at the right, pointing with his left hand to the grille of the cell, wants to have his charge finally behind bars; his entire body, with its complex variety of gestures and attitudes, conveys his urgency. John, for his part, has been modelled by the sculptor as consistent in his action: there is no hesitation or tension of opposing gestures. He is walking straight ahead, to and into his cell.

Details: 34 John and guard; 35 guard

33

PANEL XIII

John's Disciples visit him in Prison: While John was in prison, he heard from some of his disciples, who had come to visit him, that his cousin Jesus had been preaching, curing, and even raising the dead to life. Go to him, John ordered the disciples, and ask him if he is in fact the Messiah, or if we must wait still longer. Though Andrea was not able to show the figure of the imprisoned John in this panel, he has so sculpted and arranged the six visiting disciples that our attention is irresistibly drawn to the present but not visible John. As though the proportions of the prison cell and its grille were accurate, and not dictated by the area and dimensions of his panel, the sculptor has the principal visitor bending awkwardly – he must steady himself by leaning on the grille with both hands – to see and hear John. Two of the others, perhaps puzzled by the apparent hopelessness of John's question, gesture towards him behind the grille, the younger of them looking back at the other with an expression of confusion and futility. Jesus' response, in the next panel, will answer John's question and the doubts of these disciples.

Details: 41 gesturing disciples; 42 bending disciple

PANEL XV

Salome dances for Herod: As though it was not enough that Herod should live incestuously with his brother's wife, he conceived a passion for her daughter, whom the Jewish historian Josephus names as Salome. On his birthday, Herod gave a great banquet to which he invited minor princes and other officials. Salome danced for him and his guests and, in his exuberance, the Tetrarch swore an oath to reward her by giving her whatever she asked for. Salome, whom Andrea Pisano presents here as a demure young girl – young enough still, perhaps, to be present at a banquet whose guests were men and from which mature females may therefore have been excluded – went to her mother Herodias to tell her of Herod's promise and to ask what she should demand as a reward. This was Herodias' opportunity to have revenge on John for his insult to her and to aid Herod in his quandary about how to rid himself of John. (Indeed, the *Golden Legend* says that Herod and Herodias conspired that Salome should dance for him and that Herod should make his extravagant oath.) Go back, Herodias said to Salome, and tell him you want John's head, cut off and brought to you on a dish. Herod gave the order straight away. By bracketing, as it were, the figures of Herod and two of his banqueting companions with the youthful and naive figures of the musician and Salome, the sculptor has subtly emphasized by implication the horror and consequence of this scene.

Details: 45 musician; 46 Herod and Salome

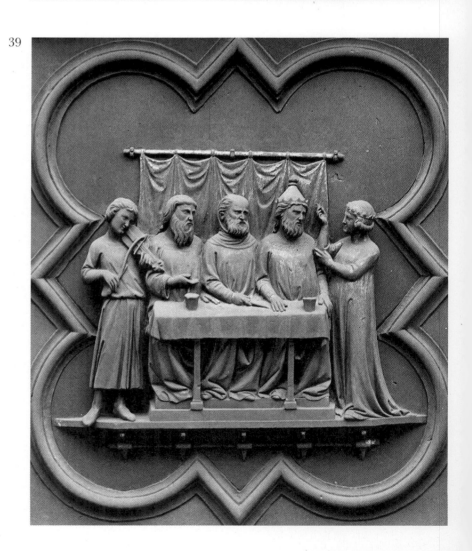

38   PANEL XIV

Christ and John's Disciples: When John's two disciples found Jesus and asked him John's question, he told them to go back to John and tell him what they had seen and heard: that the blind saw again, the lame walked, lepers were cleansed, the deaf heard, and the dead lived again. Happy, he added, perhaps as a sensitive encouragement for John, is the man who does not lose confidence in God. Then, to calm the fears of John's disciples, Jesus gives an encomium of the Baptist, among other things declaring him the greatest of all men born of women. He is, Jesus says finally, the Elijah who was to return, a reminder here of the echo of that prophet and his ravens which Andrea worked into the *John in the Wilderness* panel. Here the concentration of authority is shifted from John to Christ. In the scenes of John's preaching and baptizing, it is he who stands to the right, a single figure balanced by an opposing group. Here, John's disciples at the left, who have come to see and hear, are separated from the activity of the healing Christ by the crippled boy whose foot is grotesquely twisted, the man who, judging from the handrest on which he leans, can walk only on his knees, and the central figure, hands clasped in devotion, whose entire stance is filled with the faith that John's disciples – and John himself, perhaps – are wavering in.

Details: 43 John's disciples and Christ's followers; 44 Christ healing

40   PANEL XVI

The Beheading of John: Kneeling at the door of his cell, and wearing the camel-hair garment which by now has become one of his distinguishing characteristics, John bends low as he waits the executioner's blow. The sculptor hides most of him behind the swordsman, but shows us enough of his body, head and hands to imply that John is, at this instant, deep in prayer. The serenity of his resignation is counterbalanced by the tension in the executioner's body, as he rises on his toes to put all his weight behind the downward swing of his heavy sword. Victim and executioner are themselves contrasted with the presentation of the two onlooking guards. Curiously interested and nearly swaggering, the one at the left draws back slightly as though to be better able to see all of what is going on. His companion, who seems younger, appears indifferent, unmoved; so little is he affected by the action that he has not moved from his post outside John's cell, and still holds his lance and shield in the conventional manner.

Details: 47 soldier; 48 John kneeling

44

47

PANEL XVII

The Head of John is brought to Herod: When John's head had been cut off, it was, according to Herod's order, brought to him to be given to Salome. Herod, true to his characterization both in the Gospels and in preceding panels, is here a man still not prepared to take the consequences of his actions: he gestures broadly that the dish should be given to Salome, as though wanting to sweep away with his hand the facts and his responsibility for them. The guests, who had both earlier concentrated their attention on the young Salome, are here divided. One of them, next to Herod, appears amazed at what has been brought into the banquet hall, and points at the head, focusing his horror and consternation. His fellow guest looks quizzically at Salome, his expression and open-handed gesture implying that he sympathizes with the predicament the girl finds herself in. Salome, finally, is consistent here with the sculptor's earlier depiction of her: her coquettish innocence has brought her to a case her youth cannot deal with. She stands as far away as she can from her grisly reward, and folds her arms across her breast in confusion, puzzlement and perhaps the helpless realization of the pawn she has been in a game played by adults.

Details: 53 Salome; 54 guest; 55 Herod and the head of John

PANEL XIX

John's Disciples take away his Body: The Gospels record only that, after John's death, some of his disciples came and took away his body; no mention is made of his head, which of course was by then within Herod's palace. There is an ancient legend that Herodias, fearful that John would perhaps return to haunt and persecute her, held back the head and had it secretly buried in Jerusalem, believing that his return would be impossible if his head and body were separated in burial. Andrea not only does not follow either of these directions of conjecture in this panel, but rather goes to the extreme of showing both head and body being carried away in a manner which would be physically impossible. The viewer asks how a decapitated body and its head could be carried with such formal discipline. The line from John's crown to his feet is unbelievably straight; the first bearer on the left, seen from the back, supports the head by putting his hand beneath the cerecloths – but how does that prevent a grisly accident? The sculptor may have sacrificed verisimilitude to give himself the opportunity to create a group of funereal formality and sorrow. Each of the six bearers appears lost in grief, almost immobile, except for the movement expressed through their draped legs and their feet. By far the greatest part of their energy and activity goes into supporting their burden.

Detail: 58 John's bearers

50 PANEL XVIII

Salome brings Herodias the Head of John: Andrea Pisano sustains his scenario by having Salome take John's head from the banquet hall to another room, where she hands it over to her mother. Herodias, upright in posture but with a withdrawn and thoughtful expression, holds the dish which Salome has not yet let go of. By focusing all attention on the head in its dish held by the hands of the mother and the daughter, Andrea draws together their shared guilt and individual reactions to it. Salome kneels on one knee only, tensely leaning towards her mother to hold out the tragic prize. Now that she has been revenged, and in such a way, Herodias appears nonplussed. The eagerness with which she urged Salome to get John's head is gone; she sits here, back straight and almost stiff, with her head alone bending to consider the outcome of her earlier outrage. Salome gazes intently at her mother's face, searching perhaps for a clue as to what her reaction ought to be now that her obedience to Herodias' instructions has borne fruit. Even in death, and separated from his body, John's face has the look of the resigned but determined Precursor who was insistent that his role was to make straight the way of the One who would follow him.
Details : 56 Salome presenting the head ; 57 Herodias

52 PANEL XX

The Burial of John the Baptist: The sculptor again, and this time drastically, puts aside his earlier diligence at verisimilitude and concludes the story of his hero John by setting his burial in a contemporary context. The background architecture, the tomb itself, the attendant acolyte holding a long taper and dressed like a fourteenth-century monk – each of these details seems to indicate that Andrea Pisano had deliberately ceased chronicling, and had changed his spiritual outlook on his theme. Only the six disciples of John remain consistent, in their clothing and attitude, with Andrea's previously constant attempt to record John's history. This tension between the contemporaneity of the burial's setting and the historical fact of most of the participants may have been a deliberate device. By surrounding John's burial with details familiar to Florentines at the time he made the door, the artist was perhaps attempting to demonstrate the difference between history and legend, and how history refers to the past though legend continues to live, because of its universal and timeless meaning, into the present. It was, perhaps, more important to him to remind Florence that its Baptistery claimed the constant patronage of John the Baptist than merely to describe his life.
Detail : 59 grieving disciples

53

54

56

PANEL XXI

60

Hope: As the visual basis for his life of John the Baptist, Andrea Pisano provides two rows of panels in four columns. He combines the theological virtues – Faith, Hope, Charity – with the so-called 'cardinal' (because they are the 'hinges' on which all merit, natural or theological, depends) virtues – Prudence, Justice, Fortitude, Temperance. The eighth panel depicts Humility.

In this, the first panel of the group, Hope (*Spes*) appears as a winged female, half-rising to grasp the crown that floats above and beyond her. The virtue of hope is a characteristic which leads mankind up and beyond the present to the future, where something 'better' is looked for. This combination of expectation and amelioration is the essence of hope. Andrea's Hope, tense and straining as she is, and with her eyes not confronting the present but gazing urgently into the future, could degenerate into her opposite vice of Despair, were she not accompanied, both in practice and as here, by the coordinate virtues of Faith (the basis of things hoped for), Fortitude (unwavering endurance), and Temperance (to distinguish the appropriate from the fancied).

Details: 62 drapery; 63 head in profile

PANEL XXII

61

Faith: Andrea's Faith (*Fides*), behind her the conventional hexagonal halo shared by all her sister virtues, sits foursquare and firm, holding her two attributes of chalice and cross. The sculptor has placed her beneath the panel of Christ's baptism by John (plate 27), the first revelation in the New Testament of the Trinity. Only thus, he seems to be indicating, can man accept a concept so extravagantly beyond reason: if it does not rest on faith, it is mere absurdity. The chalice she holds, a sign of the Eucharist and of the Christian belief in salvation through Christ's blood, and the cross, the effective, material instrument of Christ's redemptive death, are separate but joined by an implication of timelessness. Faith cannot rest in the acceptance of the historical fact of the crucifixion alone, but must extend to accepting the continuing promise and effect of salvation through the Eucharist.

Detail: 64 head in profile

PANEL XXIII

Fortitude: As the foundation and support for the ideals and events chronicled in his door, Andrea Pisano portrays the cardinal, or natural, virtues. In his *Republic*, Plato had prescribed the four virtues necessary for the citizens of the ideal city-state: prudence, justice, fortitude, temperance. The early Christian Fathers adopted these natural attributes, so by Andrea's time they were long-established in the repertoire of belief. Fortitude, again a woman but whose face and bared arms emphasize her 'masculine' qualities, looks off (like Hope, above her) into the future. The club she holds, her traditional attribute, is the club of Hercules, the legendary prototype of unflagging courage, endurance and strength. Hope, Fortitude, Humility and Prudence are arranged in two opposing but coordinated pairs, so that each pair looks into the body of the door, enclosing, as it were, the symbolic dynamism of the two rows of virtues. Thematically, the direction of their gaze is consistent with, and indeed emphasizes, their individual meanings.

65

PANEL XXIV

Temperance: Her direct gaze and composed smile make this figure the embodiment of the quality she represents. From the ancient Greeks' μηδὲν ἄγαν ('nothing in excess'), through Horace's *aurea mediocritas* ('golden moderation'), temperance came in the Christian catalogue to mean an active, deliberate attitude rather than a passive withdrawn one. Temperance's attribute is the sword, whose sharp edge of discernment and discretion carries the full meaning of the virtue. The sword, however, is sheathed, and its sheath is bound with cord or, as Andrea has expressed it here, with a ribbon; thus the virtue is not easily exercised, nor can it be brought to bear impetuously. It has its own measured difficulty and though, like its personification here, an individual may have it available, 'to hand', it is to be wielded with directness and composure only.

Detail: 67 *face*

66

PANEL XXV

Charity: After Paul's encomium of charity to the Corinthians, there was nothing more to be said about this queen of the virtues, 'the greatest of these'. Andrea Pisano ends his catalogue of the theological virtues by showing Charity, as confronting as her sister Faith (plate 61), holding two of her symbols: a sphere and a cornucopia. Love, or charity, never comes to an end, says Paul, and is therefore whole and integral in itself, just as a sphere has no ending or, once it has been completed, beginning, neither inside nor outside: take away a 'part' of it and the sphere is destroyed. Similarly, Charity's unfailing quality is symbolized by her cornucopia, that ancient symbol of never-ending bounty: there is no limit or exhaustion to true charity.

PANEL XXVII

Justice: Andrea's Justice, who according to Plato regulates the work of the other three natural virtues, is open-faced, confronting and direct of gaze. Not till the late Renaissance was she shown blindfolded, which indeed had until then indicated lack of judgment (as in the blindfolded Cupid, for instance). To the ancients, and well into and after the sculptor's time, Justice was clear-sighted, impartial. This quality combines the discernment of Temperance's sword, here unsheathed and poised for use, and the scales, which had been introduced as one of Justice's attributes by the Romans and which indicate the balance of her consideration and conclusive judgment. This panel closes the literally four-square arrangement Andrea Pisano has devised of the confronting virtues – Faith, Charity, Temperance, Justice. They are, he appears to imply, the qualities which, of all those in these two bottom rows, most have to do with the 'here and now', men's daily, immediate life and actions, and least – though obviously to some measure – referring to either past or future. In concert with their sister virtues, as Plato said, they make it possible for the good citizen to influence and modify his present behaviour, so that his future may be better regulated.

Detail: 72 face

69 PANEL XXVI

Humility: Among all Andrea Pisano's virtues, Humility is, perhaps, the least touching, almost ungraspable in her allusiveness. As difficult to portray as she is to acquire, Humility in Andrea's presentation is aloof, enigmatic, self-contained. Just as pride is the source of all vice, so humility must be the foundation of any attempt at virtuous living, requiring as it does a clear-sighted discipline and recognition of one's own deficiencies. For this reason, perhaps, Andrea has included her here as a bridge between the theological and cardinal virtues. Part of the catalogue of neither, humility is nevertheless essential to both; similarly, just as the viewer of the door must recognize and acknowledge her presence here, so the individual striving for virtue must humbly accept that the theological virtues can only be genuine if based on the natural, or cardinal, virtues.

71 PANEL XXVIII

Prudence: Of all Andrea's panels of the virtues, this one of Prudence, the last of the cardinal virtues here, is perhaps the most complex in its symbolism. In her left hand she holds a book, token of that other virtue, Wisdom, who is not portrayed but who is alluded to by the book: 'I Wisdom dwell with Prudence.' Wisdom is again recalled by the serpent in Prudence's right hand, a reminder of the attitude expressed in Christ's admonition to his disciples to be 'as wise as serpents'. Essentially, however, prudence as a human trait, and not an anthropomorphized allegorical concept, is a characteristic that combines memory – the past – and foresight – the future. Those acts are prudential which have an eye to remembered experience and predictable consequences. For that reason, therefore, Prudence here is double-faced: the woman who, like Memory, brings the past into the present is joined with the conventionally male characteristic of planning, 'keeping an eye on the future'. Altogether, the sculptor has contrived with balance and uncluttered sensitivity to make his Prudence very far indeed from that timidity her name too often suggests.
Details: 73 snake and hand; 74 male head; 75 female face; 76 male face

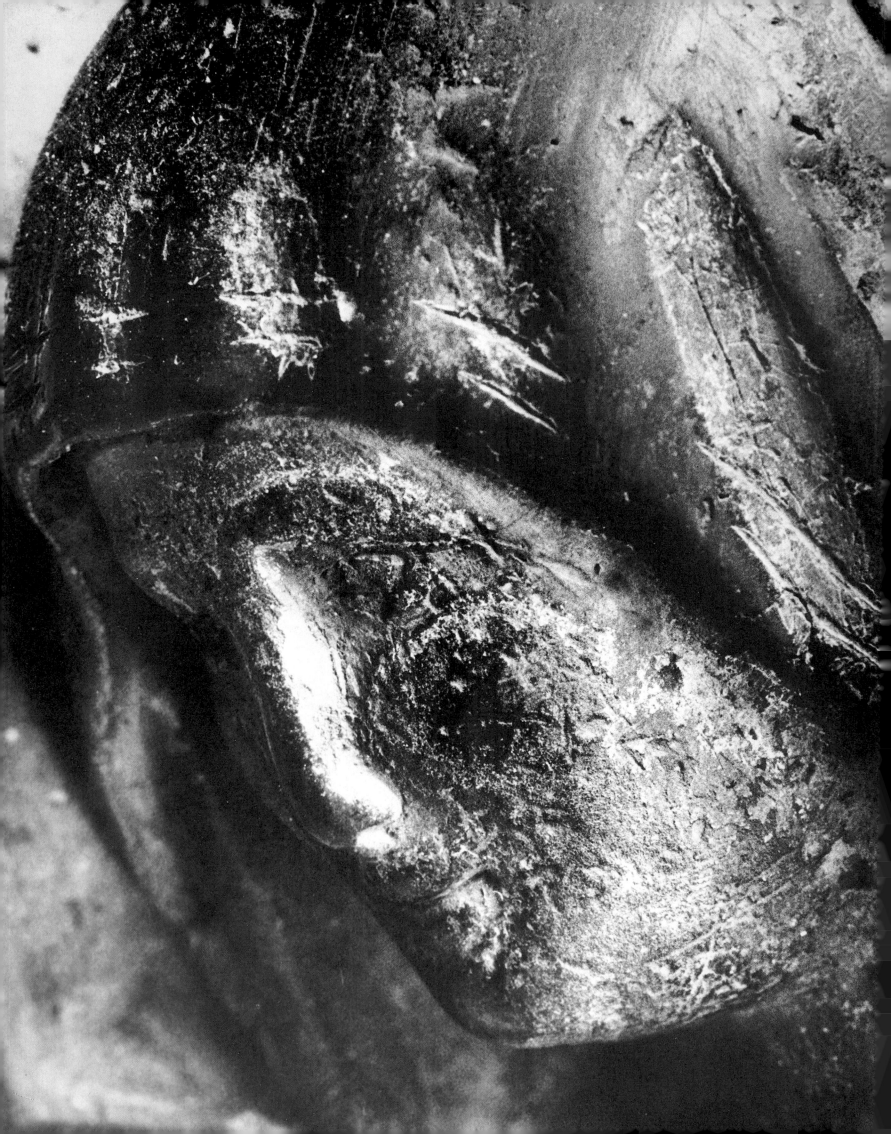

THE NORTH DOOR

LORENZO GHIBERTI

78

THE NORTH DOOR

XXV	XXVI	XXVII	XXVIII
XXI	XXII	XXIII	XXIV
XVII	XVIII	XIX	XX
XIII	XIV	XV	XVI
IX	X	XI	XII
V	VI	VII	VIII
I	II	III	IV

In 1401, the guild of merchants called the Arte di Calimala, having decided that their *bel San Giovanni* deserved an appropriate follow-up to Andrea Pisano's splendid door, invited submissions for doors to be placed at the Baptistery's north and south sides. The proposal was that the South Door should illustrate scenes from the Gospels, and the North Door should recall the history narrated in the Old Testament. Thus, as it turned out, Andrea's chronicle of John the Baptist would be enhanced by reinforcing his role as last of the prophets of the old dispensation, and precursor of the Christ of the Gospels.

Of the seven artists involved in the Calimala's competition, Filippo Brunelleschi and Lorenzo Ghiberti, the youngest in the group and each only just past twenty, were selected for final choice. Ghiberti, who had had no or very little experience, was chosen to do the Gospels door, with the option that he would later do the Old Testament door as well.

Between about 1404, when he assembled his assistants, and 1424, after the door had been cast, gilded and hung, Ghiberti devoted his time, energy and concentration to the work. Except for its change of theme – scenes from the life of Christ – the door was to follow the pattern of Andrea Pisano's door: four rows of columns, each of seven panels enclosing quatrefoils. By the time Ghiberti began work, it had been decided that Andrea's door should be moved, and the new door placed not on the south but on the east. It was itself later moved to make way for Ghiberti's 'Gates of Paradise', assuming in 1452 its final position as the North Door.

Ghiberti literally and figuratively based his interpretation of Christ's life on the Fathers of the Church, four of whom – Augustine, Jerome, Gregory and Ambrose – make up the bottom row of panels. Above them, as recording intermediaries between the life of Christ and his action, and the interpretation of his doctrine by the Fathers, are the four Evangelists, John, Matthew, Luke and Mark. The sequence of events on the door begins at the *Annunciation*, in the panel above John, and runs across the door from left to right in ascending order. The story flows, as it were, according to the 'upward path of salvation'. Ghiberti emphasizes the role and position of Mary in this history by making her the principal figure in the *Annunciation* and the *Pentecost*, the first and last panels in the chronicle proper.

Throughout, Ghiberti appears to depend for his facts and attitude more on John's Gospel than on the other three. Thus, for example, he places the *Expulsion of the Money-Changers* scene before the *Entry into Jerusalem*, following John's sequence and not the other Evangelists'. More than that, however, by this predilection for John's story, Ghiberti is able to stress Christ's human characteristics, so that in the *Last Supper*, of all the events on that occasion that he might have portrayed, he chooses to show the head of John, who refers to himself as 'the disciple Jesus loved', reclining on Christ's bosom. Equally, in the *Crucifixion*, Ghiberti has the dead Christ accompanied by John and Mary only, a group mentioned only by John in his account.

Altogether, Ghiberti's Christ is a dignified, resigned, almost aloof Messiah, whose attitude and behaviour have consistently an overtone of sadness and separateness. Only once, in the *Expulsion*, has Ghiberti allowed him to manifest an obvious emotion – in this instance fierce and punishing rage – though the artist's preference for John's narrative might have permitted him a more obvious display of feeling in, for example, the *Raising of Lazarus*, John's account of which is the most moving.

Once they had been cast, by the 'lost wax' process, and gilded by a method in which gold dust was mixed with mercury which was then sublimated in a furnace, the enormous – 15 by 8 feet (4.6 by 2.4 metres) – and heavy doors were hung in place. After some twenty years of work on them Ghiberti, who was now only in his early forties, had accomplished a masterpiece – but he was to go on to at least another.

The captions to colour plates 79–86 are on page 105.

PANEL I

Augustine: Bishop of Hippo in North Africa and probably one of the Church's most celebrated saints as well as one of Western civilization's most influential writers, Augustine (354–430) is paired with Jerome by Ghiberti as the only one of the Fathers attentive to two books or documents. In Augustine's case, Ghiberti may be alluding to the Saint's dictum that 'The Old Testament is the New Testament veiled; the New Testament is the Old Testament revealed', so that each of the two books of the Christian Bible he is here comparing depends upon and implies the other.

Details: 91 hand of St Augustine; 93 head and torso

PANEL III

Gregory the Great: The only pope among these four Fathers of the Church, Gregory (540–604) formulated the early liturgy of the Latin Church and was responsible for the establishment of what is known as 'Gregorian chant', or plainsong. Ghiberti portrays him in the papal regalia, most distinctive of which is the tiara, the beehive-shaped headdress encircled by a crown symbolizing the pope's sovereignty. By Ghiberti's time it had become a triple crown, but he chose to show the simpler early form.

Detail: 96 profile of St Gregory

88 PANEL II

Jerome: A Dalmatian by birth, Jerome (342–420) went at the middle of his life to live in Bethlehem, and devoted the rest of his days to translating the Old and New Testaments into Latin, in what is known as the Vulgate version. Ghiberti shows him, a venerable but not yet old man, busy at that task. The monastic robes in which he is clothed are an allusion to the austerity and dedication of his young manhood when he withdrew into the desert and lived as a hermit for four years.

Details: *92 hand of St Jerome; 94 head; 95 head in profile*

90 PANEL IV

Ambrose: Bishop of Milan and great champion of orthodoxy against the Arian heresy, Ambrose (340–397) was known as both statesman and commentator. In his writings he stressed the role of human sin and divine grace, and it was he whose influence as teacher and friend converted Augustine.

Ambrose closes Ghiberti's catalogue of the Fathers of the Western Church. In the arrangement here, showing the four Doctors and then the four Evangelists, Ghiberti follows a convention that coupled the two groups as first promulgators and first interpreters of Christ's teaching.

Detail: *97 head and shoulders of St Ambrose*

91

92

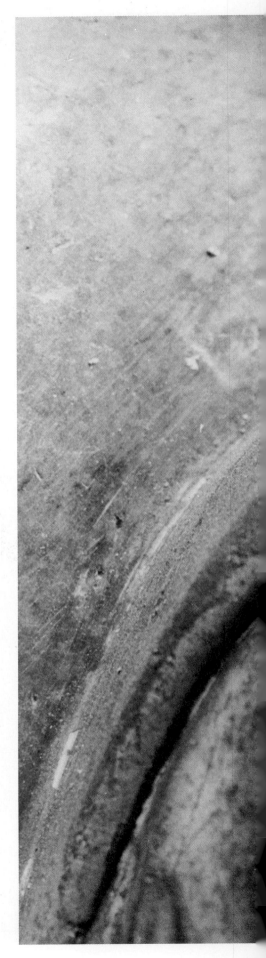

John: The first in Ghiberti's row of Evangelists, John was one of the first apostles to be called by Jesus. He was the 'disciple Jesus loved', and Ghiberti chose to emphasize that special favour in his panel of the Last Supper (plate 150). In addition to his Gospel, John is traditionally believed to have written the Apocalypse, or Book of Revelation, in exile on the Aegean island of Patmos. Ghiberti depicts John here as though rapt in one of the many visions which he transcribed to make up the Apocalypse. He is attended by an eagle, the symbol of the unearthliness of his inspiration and one of the four creatures he himself describes as surrounding the throne of God, as well as, with the ox, man (or winged man) and lion, one of the creatures traditionally assigned as symbols of the four Evangelists.

Details: 102 St John's bowed head; 103 the eagle

Luke: Luke, the only one of the Evangelists who had not been one of Jesus' twelve disciples and had probably not even known him, is customarily symbolized or, as here shown by Ghiberti, accompanied by an ox. As the ox was an animal of sacrifice, the allusion is to the beginning of Luke's Gospel, in which he recounts Zacharias' sacrifice of incense at the time of the annunciation of the Baptist's future conception and birth. Equally, because he needed to depend on other sources than his own experience in writing his account of Jesus' life, Luke is the only one of Ghiberti's Evangelists shown as though comparing or consulting two documents, one perhaps his own Gospel, the other a source.

Details: 106 St Luke's documents; 108 head of St Luke; 109 the ox

99　PANEL VI

Matthew: Ghiberti chooses to portray the author of the first Gospel as though attended by an angel, while his traditional symbol – based on John's Apocalypse as well as Ezekiel's 'four creatures' – is a man, or winged man. As Matthew's Gospel is, of the four, the one which concentrates on the human character of Christ, and on the details of his human activities, the figure of a man became appropriated to him as his symbol as Evangelist of the Incarnation.
Details: 104 angel; 105 profile of St Matthew

101　PANEL VIII

Mark: Mark's Gospel opens with John the Baptist, the 'voice of one crying in the wilderness', and so his symbolic beast is the lion, here shown winged and so divinized, which roars and proclaims its presence in the desert. Ghiberti has placed this panel showing Mark – the four panels of the Evangelists follow no traditional sequence – beneath that of the young Christ among the doctors in the Temple, as though to allude to Jesus' first public proclamation of his mission on that occasion.
Details: 107 hand and Gospel of St Mark; 110 St Mark's head; 111 the lion

109

111

PANEL IX

The Annunciation: Of all representations of the announcement by the angel Gabriel to Mary that she was to be the mother of the Messiah, Ghiberti's in a special way reproduces the atmosphere of the event as described in Luke's Gospel, the only one of the four to record it. Ghiberti naturally enough focuses attention on Mary: Gabriel leans towards and salutes her; God the Father bends down from heaven to release the Holy Spirit, portrayed in the conventional form of a dove. Mary's attitude, however, surprises us: this obviously frightened young woman is not the stereotyped, instantly submissive 'Handmaid of the Lord' that she has, particularly in modern times, become. Ghiberti, rather, takes his cue from Luke, and reproduces the moment when, immediately Gabriel has appeared and saluted her as 'full of grace', Mary draws back 'terrified'. Indeed, her naiveté and innocent terror are in sharp but comprehensible contrast to the reaction of Pisano's Zacharias when, shortly before, he too was visited by the same Gabriel who brought a similar message (plate 10). Zacharias the priest was an old man, not easily startled perhaps by God's working and basically sceptical of Gabriel's news. Ghiberti's Mary, on the other hand, appears to react from faith rather than experience, and in her self-shielding gesture she is implied as somehow apprehending the gravity involved in her visit from an angel.

Details: 116 dove; 117 Mary; 118 angel

PANEL XI

The Adoration of the Magi: Ghiberti's three Magi, wise men from the East, crowd into one side of this panel with excitement and wonder. One of their retinue, a Negro, has brought his pet monkey. Of the three principal visitors, the first, and perhaps therefore the eldest and most exalted, raises his head, from what Ghiberti by that posture implies was a prostration, to kiss the foot of the Child Christ. His two companions wait behind him, holding their shares of the triple gift of gold, frankincense and myrrh which Matthew says they brought and which are traditionally understood as symbols of the royalty (gold), divinity (frankincense), and Passion (myrrh for embalming) of Christ. In this visit of Caspar, Melchior and Balthasar, the three representatives of the Gentile 'East' – though the monkey and its black owner are consistent with the tradition that one of the three was a Negro – custom has seen the fulfilment of Isaiah's prophecy that all peoples would come out of the East to worship the Messiah, bringing gold and frankincense as gifts of homage. The manifestation – Epiphany – of Christ to the Gentiles implemented that aspect of his role as Messiah, who came not only for Israel but for all mankind. Ghiberti directs all emphasis and attention, then, to the child, who appears excited by the visitors but is restrained by Mary, sitting here in what is a sensitively suggested secondary role, while Joseph remains, perhaps puzzled, in the background and half hidden by the column he leans against.

Details: 124 wise man; 125 Negro and monkey; 126 kneeling wise man

113 PANEL X

The Nativity: Like her cousin Elizabeth in Andrea Pisano's record of John the Baptist's birth (plate 13), Ghiberti's Mary lies quietly and calmly here, in contemplation of her Child. The infant Christ – again, like Andrea's infant John, looking considerably older than a newborn – smiles down at the ox and the ass, those two conventional Beasts of the Nativity first mentioned as present by an eighth-century pseudo-gospel. Isaiah's statement that the ox knows its master and the ass its stall was later seen as a prophecy of the Jews' inability to accept Christ as the Messiah. Ghiberti – perhaps in order to give logic to including here the angel's announcement of Christ's birth to the shepherds, who were 'living in the fields' – places the event in what is apparently the open air, though there are suggestions of the traditional cave of the Nativity in the formation of the rocks, and the shelves on which Mary and the child recline. He further condenses the sequence of events into the space of his panel by having his announcing angel's arms outstretched in such a gesture that the left draws the startled shepherds into the scene pointed at by his right. Characteristically, Joseph, the husband of Mary, does not enter into the action but, because his presence is recorded in the Gospels, he is here, either brooding or sleeping.
Details: 119 angel; 120 Mary's head; 121 infant Christ; 122 ox and ass; 123 Joseph

115 PANEL XII

Christ among the Doctors: When Jesus was twelve years old, he had gone up to Jerusalem with Mary and Joseph, whose practice it was to spend the Passover in that city. Once the holiday had passed, the parents began their return journey to Nazareth, taking it for granted that the boy was among their friends and relatives travelling in the caravan. When they discovered his absence, however, they returned to Jerusalem and, after three days, finally found him in the Temple, discussing the Law with the priests and wise men. This is the moment Ghiberti has caught here: Mary, now dressed as a matron in a headdress similar to that worn by Bethlehemite women (to be brought back to Europe by the Crusaders and exaggerated into the hennin, or 'steeple' headdress), combines in her attitude relief at having found the boy, consternation at his apparent indifference to her concern, and something of a majestic resignation to the knowledge that, no matter his true nature, he must also, like all maturing young men, begin to lead his own life. Joseph, as usual, looks down in apparently uncomprehending but submissive thought, while the bearded elder seated before Mary's feet appears to look up at her in eagerness to see the mother of such a child. Though he has succeeded in focusing all attention, both of the viewer and of the personages in the panel, on the central figure of the young Christ, Ghiberti has modelled the boy and his mother so that they are aware of both the occasion and each other's feelings.
Details: 127 elder with book; 128 priests; 129 elder in profile; 130 Mary and Joseph

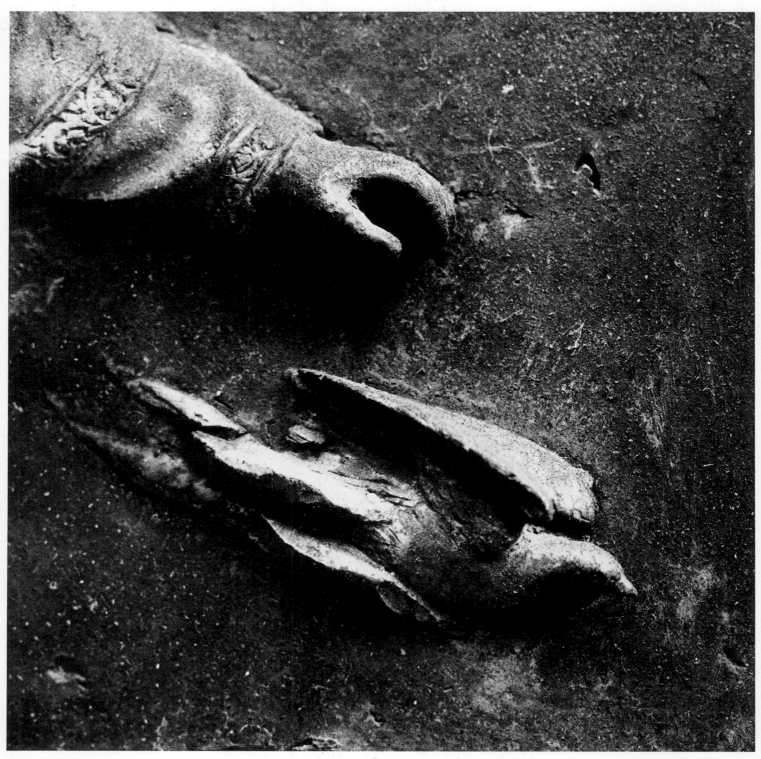

116

117

119

120

122

Christ is baptized by John: Because Ghiberti's theme was the life of Christ, his treatment of this incident has a thematic viewpoint different from Andrea Pisano's panel of the same event (plate 27). Most noticeably, perhaps, Ghiberti lays heavy emphasis on the occasion's spiritual, indeed divine, meaning by substituting for the earlier single attending angel a group of those heavenly beings, busy talking among themselves about what is going on. One of them is not winged, but we know, by Ghiberti's subtle implication, that they are all angels. Equally, this St John steps back as far as he can to the border of the panel, by that motion deflecting attention on to its central figure of Christ. Inevitably, because the Gospel history requires it, the dove of the Holy Spirit hovers over Christ. But the combination of the angels' sacred conversation, Ghiberti's clear decision to portray Christ without a halo (a decision he sustains throughout this door) and his omission of the rays of light that Andrea has stream from the dove underlines the essentially spiritual import of this occasion, the first manifestation of the Three Persons of the Trinity.

Details : 135 Christ baptized ; 136 John

The Expulsion of the Money-Changers from the Temple : According to three Evangelists, this event took place after Jesus' entry into Jerusalem ; John alone records it as having occurred long before that and, indeed, before the occasions depicted by Ghiberti in his next three panels. Why Ghiberti's programme took advantage of John's variation from the other Evangelists can only be conjectured, but the juxtaposition of this panel with the previous one creates a dramatic contrast of the ways in which Christ confronted evil. In the *Temptation*, he stands firm and resolutely rejects the true absurdity of Satan's suggestions. When he came to the Temple, however, and found that the legitimate concessions to provide worshippers with coins and small animals for sacrifice had been so abused as to make the Temple porch a place of squalor, filth and noise, he reacted in violent anger. This is the instant Ghiberti reproduces, evoking the fury of Christ, who raises one hand above his head and with the other outstretched arm shoves the huddled and confused merchants away. In their urgency to escape, they have knocked down one young man, who raises his hand to shield himself against the person who is about to trample him. Only the woman farthest to the right looks back at the outraged Christ, as though puzzled by his behaviour.

Details : 139 merchant ; 140 fallen man ; 141 Christ ; 142 crowd in the Temple

132   PANEL XIV

The Temptation in the Wilderness: We know from Matthew, Mark and Luke that, after his baptism by John, Jesus himself withdrew into the wilderness to undergo initiatory temptation. Fasting forty days and nights, Jesus was first challenged by Satan to turn stone into bread, a taunt he deflected by reminding that formerly greatest of the angels that man 'does not live by bread alone'. At this point Satan attempted to turn Scripture to his own ends by urging Jesus to cast himself from a mountain, for God the Father would save him by putting him in 'His angels' charge'; to this Jesus replied, perhaps sarcastically in view of Satan's tragic downfall, 'You must not put God to the test.' Finally, and from the profundity of his own pride, Satan invited Jesus to bow down before him, as before God, in return for all the riches and splendour of the world. 'Begone, Satan,' was Jesus' last response, with a gesture Ghiberti reproduces here in counterpoint to Mary's very similar gesture in the *Annunciation* panel (plate 112). There, she shielded herself from the holy terror of an angelic apparition; Christ here casts away Satan, quite a different sort of angel, with his bat-wings and twisted horns. Among the angels behind Christ, who Matthew says appeared to look after him, is one who folds his arms across his breast, in resignation perhaps; he will appear again when Ghiberti records occasions when Christ's mission was tested by suffering or temptation.
Details: 137 Satan; 138 Christ

134   PANEL XVI

Christ walks upon the Water: After the miracle of feeding thousands of people with five loaves and two fishes, Jesus told his disciples to sail across to the other side of the Sea of Galilee, where he would join them. They had not been long out to sea, however, when a storm rose suddenly and violently, and the disciples became very frightened. Jesus saw this, and began to walk across the water to them, though they were terrified to see him, and thought it was a spectre. To reassure them, he called out, 'Do not be afraid – it is I.' At that, Peter, ever impetuous and eager for signs and miracles, said that if it was the Lord he would make it possible for him to walk over the waves, and he stepped from the boat. When the wind rose, however, Peter's temerity deserted him, and he began to sink, calling on Jesus to save him. Ghiberti shows the two at that instant, Jesus reaching out to touch Peter's hands outstretched in supplication and panic. In the boat, the others are either busy navigating it, with its furled sails, in the tempest, looking up at the sky in the hope the storm will soon pass, or, like those at the stern, realizing the miracle they have just witnessed and huddled in conversation about it.

In this row, Ghiberti has paired along the outer margins of the door two incidents involving Christ and water, and retains and carries forward his consistent portrait of the serene Christ, while contrasting the life-giving baptismal waters of the Jordan with the turbulence of the stormy Sea of Galilee.
Details: 143 disciple and rigging; 144 Christ; 145 disciples in the stern; 146 head of disciple

145

PANEL XVII

The Transfiguration: Jesus took Peter, James and John up to Mount Tabor, so that they might all be alone and pray together. While Jesus prayed, his face shone like the sun, and his clothing became white as lightning. Suddenly, Moses and Elijah appeared, each of them standing on one side of the Lord. During this moment, the three apostles were overcome by the splendour and numinosity of the scene. Peter, however, who quickly established himself as a man rash in speech and action, a characterization Ghiberti remains faithful to in these panels, burst out and proposed that he should build three tabernacles on the spot, one each for Jesus, Moses and Elijah. At that moment – Peter's outbursts were generally followed by an instant change of ambience – a bright cloud appeared, from which a voice was heard referring to Jesus as 'Son'. The apostles, by now perhaps almost overcome by fear, shrank and hid their faces. This is the instant Ghiberti has chosen to reproduce of the event. While Jesus stands in the calm attitude Ghiberti consistently gives him, Moses and Elijah, respectively representing the Law and the Prophets, flank him, who is the focus of all their attention. The cringing apostles – we recognize Peter in the middle from the previous panel – are overcome by what they have witnessed.

Details: 151 Moses; 152 Christ; 153 Elijah; 154 disciple; 155 disciple turning away

PANEL XIX

The Entry into Jerusalem: From Bethany, Jesus made his way towards Jerusalem. When people there heard he was coming, the news of the raising of Lazarus fanned their enthusiasm, and they waited for him with excitement. Jesus, however, was determined not to arrive as an earthly king, but to demonstrate the messianic prophecies, so he came riding on a donkey's colt as Zachariah the prophet had foretold: 'See, O daughter of Zion, your king is coming, mounted on the colt of a donkey.' The people of Jerusalem – Ghiberti includes its towers in the background – came out to meet and escort him into the city, and some of them spread their garments in the road before him. Ghiberti reproduces faithfully the atmosphere of the Gospel narratives, even to the sensitive reminder, in Jesus' awkwardly stretched right leg and foot, that a donkey is too small a mount for a grown man comfortably to sit astride. But of all the people he has filled this panel with, Ghiberti seems to call the viewer's special attention to the man almost precisely in the middle, beneath the larger of the towers. He alone, in the whole crowd, is not talking to anyone else but concentrates all of his attention on Jesus, perhaps appraising him for himself, independently of his neighbours' enthusiasm. Out of all this tumult, only he, Ghiberti seems to indicate, may be aware that such an entry into Jerusalem cannot go without consequences.

Details: 159 head of Jesus and crowd; 160 boy and donkey

148   PANEL XVIII

The Raising of Lazarus: Jesus had three friends, Lazarus and his sisters Martha and Mary, who lived in Bethany, a village to the east of Jerusalem. Lazarus fell ill and Martha, the elder sister who has traditionally become a symbol of the person 'busy about many things', sent a message to Jesus that his friend was ill. By the time it was possible for Jesus to reach Bethany, however, Lazarus was dead and had been in his tomb for four days. Martha reproached Jesus, saying that if he had been there her brother would not have died, and Jesus, moved by her grief, asked to be taken to the tomb where, John says, 'Jesus wept.' Ordering those standing by to remove the stone sealing the tomb, Jesus called out to his friend to come forth, which he did, wearing the grave clothes. Ghiberti captures the profound feeling of this moment, with Lazarus just barely stepped from his coffin, startled perhaps by this call back to life. The bystanding apostles are, as usual, eagerly discussing among themselves what has happened. Of the sisters, Martha is modelled by Ghiberti in an ambivalent way: is she thanking Jesus for the return of her brother, or is she still kneeling in supplication, not yet turned to see the risen Lazarus? In the prostrate Mary, Ghiberti has conflated Lazarus' resurrection with another incident, when she anointed Christ's feet and wiped them with her hair. Thus Ghiberti, by using Mary here to recall that other scene, amplifies the panel's atmosphere of death, resurrection, friendship, sorrow, penitence, humility.
Details: 156 robed man; 157 Lazarus, disciples, Jesus; 158 Mary

150   PANEL XX

The Last Supper: When Ghiberti came to model this panel, he might have chosen one of several incidents at the Last Supper: the institution of the Eucharist, perhaps, or the moment when Jesus acknowledged that Judas would betray him, or Jesus washing the apostles' feet. Equally, he might have been expected to position Jesus in the middle of the row of apostles facing out of the panel; instead, Jesus sits at the extreme left of that row with the head of John, the Evangelist who in his account of this last meeting refers to himself as 'the disciple Jesus loved', on his breast. There is, then, surprisingly – for Ghiberti is a master of the dramatic – little action in this panel, and it is puzzling in the apparent immobility of its composition, until we compare it with Andrea Pisano's panel in which the disciples of John the Baptist take away his body (plate 51). Aside from the obvious differences of architecture, number of people, event, etc., Ghiberti's composition here is too similar to Andrea's to be accidental. Nor does it appear unreasonable to recall that the only 'horizontal' head in each panel is of someone named John. One explanation – ignoring any conjectured homage, tribute, or compliment to Andrea – may be that Ghiberti, faced with the special problem of fitting the required thirteen figures into the area of his quatrefoil, adopted a schema already used by Andrea.
Details: 161 head of Christ; 162 profile of disciple at right

153

155

156

157

158

162

1

PANEL XXI

The Agony in the Garden: After the Last Supper, Jesus went into the Garden of Gethsemane with all of his disciples. He left eight of them – Judas had by now gone off to effect the next step in his betrayal – and took Peter, James and John with him to pray. A great sadness came over him, and deep distress, and he prayed that the chalice of suffering he foresaw might pass from him, but nevertheless submitted himself to his Father's will. While this agony proceeded, the three disciples he had brought as companions fell asleep, thus leaving him in his solitude. Here Ghiberti reproduces the 'angel of resignation' who first appeared in the *Temptation* panel (plate 132). With its arms folded across its breast, it hovers near to Jesus, attentive and comforting, but nonetheless indicating the need for resignation and abandonment to what was to come.

Details: 167, 168, 169 sleeping disciples; 170 angel with Christ

PANEL XXIII

The Flagellation: Again, as in the case of the *Expulsion*, Ghiberti has altered the Gospel narrative's sequence, to have this episode precede the next, which it ought historically to follow. History in this case is based on Roman practice, in that scourging was the usual Roman precedent to crucifixion; in Ghiberti's sequence, of course, Jesus has yet to be condemned by Pilate to crucifixion. Whatever Ghiberti's purpose in this altered sequence, the panel remains perhaps the most moving of the door because of the central figure of Christ. The artist has contrived to isolate him in his humiliation and pain, but continues the earlier characterization of Jesus as patient, resigned and unflinching.

Details: 171, 172 flagellators; 173 Christ

172

171

173

PANEL XXV

The Way to Calvary: With the towers of Jerusalem in the background, as they had been when Ghiberti depicted his entry into the city, Jesus carries his cross to the place of execution, Golgotha, the 'Hill of the Skull'. Surrounded by guards and soldiers, he bears the cross (its shaft bent only in recent years) in an awkward and ungainly way, and indeed seems lost in resignation rather than suffering. Ghiberti concentrates the torment, and grief at what what is to come, in the group of women at the panel's left. Mary, in the centre, is wrapped in and encumbered by her garments as though they were symbols of her grief. Ghiberti shows her accompanied, on her right, by the youthful John, the 'disciple whom Jesus loved' and the future Evangelist and author of the Apocalypse. Behind them are four other figures; the one to the right of Mary is, perhaps, Mary Magdalene, who has already anointed Jesus' body in preparation for his death.

Detail: 180 Christ with cross

PANEL XXVII

The Resurrection: Ghiberti's risen Christ completes the logic of the artist's consistent characterization of Jesus: alone, with the only possible witnesses to the Resurrection deep in sleep, he rises from his tomb on Sunday morning in single-minded composure and aloofness. It is true, of course, that neither in the Gospels nor in any other records is there an eye-witness account of that event, upon which alone all Christianity is based: the pertinent Gospel narratives report the effect on those, Mary Magdalene for example, who went to visit the tomb after Jesus' death and found it empty. Ghiberti, nevertheless, constrained as he was to include the Resurrection in his programme, makes good use of the Jesus he has thus far depicted by showing him here in solitary triumph and transformation, while the Roman guards – ordered by Pilate to watch the tomb because it was feared Jesus' disciples might steal his body and claim he had fulfilled his promise to rise from the dead – sprawl in what Ghiberti means to be deep sleep. Thus in his final panel of events in Christ's life, Ghiberti brings to a climactic and logical conclusion the character of Christ as he saw it: by capitalizing on the Gospels' implication that only faith can persuade us that the Resurrection actually happened, he repeats conclusively, in every sense of that word, his image of Christ as necessarily unique and solitary in the messiahship he declared was his.

Detail: 182 Christ risen

177 PANEL XXVI

The Crucifixion: Consistent with his obvious preference for John's Gospel narrative of the events of Jesus' life, Ghiberti recalls the death of the crucified Jesus with only, of humans, Mary and John present. Before he died, Jesus had put Mary into John's care, and it is as though to boast of that that this Evangelist is the only one of the four Gospel writers to include her in his account of Jesus' death. Ghiberti's attendant angels at first appear conventionally grief-stricken. The one on the right, however, tears its garments in a traditional gesture of grief and mourning, a gesture which also recalls the equally traditional rending of a garment on hearing a blasphemy, a charge which had been brought against Jesus: this angel, certainly the more moved of the two, rends its garments at the blasphemy involved in the execution of Jesus, believed by Ghiberti and his fellow Christians to be God Incarnate.
Detail: 181 Christ on the cross

179 PANEL XXVIII

Pentecost: This panel commemorates an event not described in the Gospels, but recorded in the Acts of the Apostles, written by Luke as a chronicle of the apostles' lives and actions after the ascension of Jesus. After that event, Luke says, all the apostles, and Mary, returned to Jerusalem to the 'upper room where they were staying', and joined in continuous prayer. After ten days, on the feast of Pentecost, the room was filled with a sound like a powerful wind from heaven, and tongues of fire came to rest on the head of each of them. They were, Luke declares, filled with the Holy Spirit and began to speak in foreign languages. During this time there were devout men, from every known nation and speaking many different languages, in Jerusalem. When the apostles began to preach, every man heard the message and understood it as though in his own language.

Ghiberti's rather formal Pentecost appears to overlook much of the excitement of this event, though the figures standing at the door of the house express a certain, if mild, curiosity. Instead, the artist ends his description of the path of salvation by focusing on Mary, who was necessarily the principal figure of the *Annunciation*: as she was there, and on that occasion, the object of the particular attention of the Holy Spirit, so here she is similarly singled out. She is flanked by two balanced groups of six apostles each, indicating Ghiberti's care to include in their number Matthias, who had been chosen to replace Judas, and who was therefore present at Pentecost.
Detail: 183 figures in doorway

183

186

187

188

189

193

194

THE GATES
OF PARADISE

THE
EAST
DOOR

LORENZO
GHIBERTI

196

THE EAST DOOR

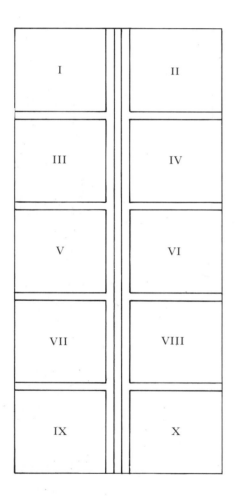

By the time Ghiberti had finished the Gospels door, it was taken for granted – despite the great time it had taken him to finish that project – that the option on his doing the third door for the Baptistery would be taken up. In 1425, the Arte di Calimala proceeded to give him a firm commission.

It had been established that the final door would illustrate scenes from the Old Testament. Ghiberti expanded his story by dividing the physical area into ten panels only, some of which include as many as five or six events. In his autobiography, he stresses his innovations in naturalism and perspective:

> I took great pains to observe all the rules of proportion and, as far as lay in my power, to imitate nature in just relationships and contours. In some stories I introduced nigh on a hundred figures.... Truly I work with the greatest diligence and love. There were ten stories altogether and all the architectural settings introduced were in perspective, and so true to life that they looked like sculpture in the round seen from the right distance. They are carried out in very low relief and the figures visible on the nearer planes are bigger than those on the distant ones, just as they appear in real life.

The narrative on the door begins with *Genesis* in the upper left-hand corner and is to be read as though the two leaves together were a page in a book: left to right, top to bottom. In his approach to the story of the Old Testament, Ghiberti emphasizes two themes: the love or conflict between brothers, and the preference so often shown by Old Testament fathers, and indeed by Yahweh himself, to younger brothers. This emphasis is never forced, nor does it distort the story Ghiberti has set out to reproduce, but he has managed, in contrast to the North Door where he appears to concentrate on Christ's isolation, to pick out of the long and complicated history of the Old Testament one thread of consummate importance: if the Israelites were to survive in their special preference by Yahweh, they had to be united despite conflict, and were obliged to allow power and authority to find its place in the hands of the young and untested. Perhaps Ghiberti's most convincing example of this attitude is in his *David* panel. Of all the events in that king's life – betrayal of a friend, adultery, composition of the Psalms, dancing before the Ark, etc. – Ghiberti focuses on a single incident, the young shepherd's slaying of Goliath and his triumphant acclaim by the Israelites for that deed, while King Saul swaggers in his chariot in the background.

When the door was finished the Florentines decided that it should have pride of place on the east side of the Baptistery, and Ghiberti's first door was moved. By 1452 it was in place. To Vasari Ghiberti's door was 'the finest masterpiece in the world whether among the ancients or the moderns', and Michelangelo, whose judgment he valued above all else, pronounced it worthy to grace the entrance to Paradise.

The captions to colour plates 197–221 are on page 225.

198

207

208

212

214

13

215

217

218

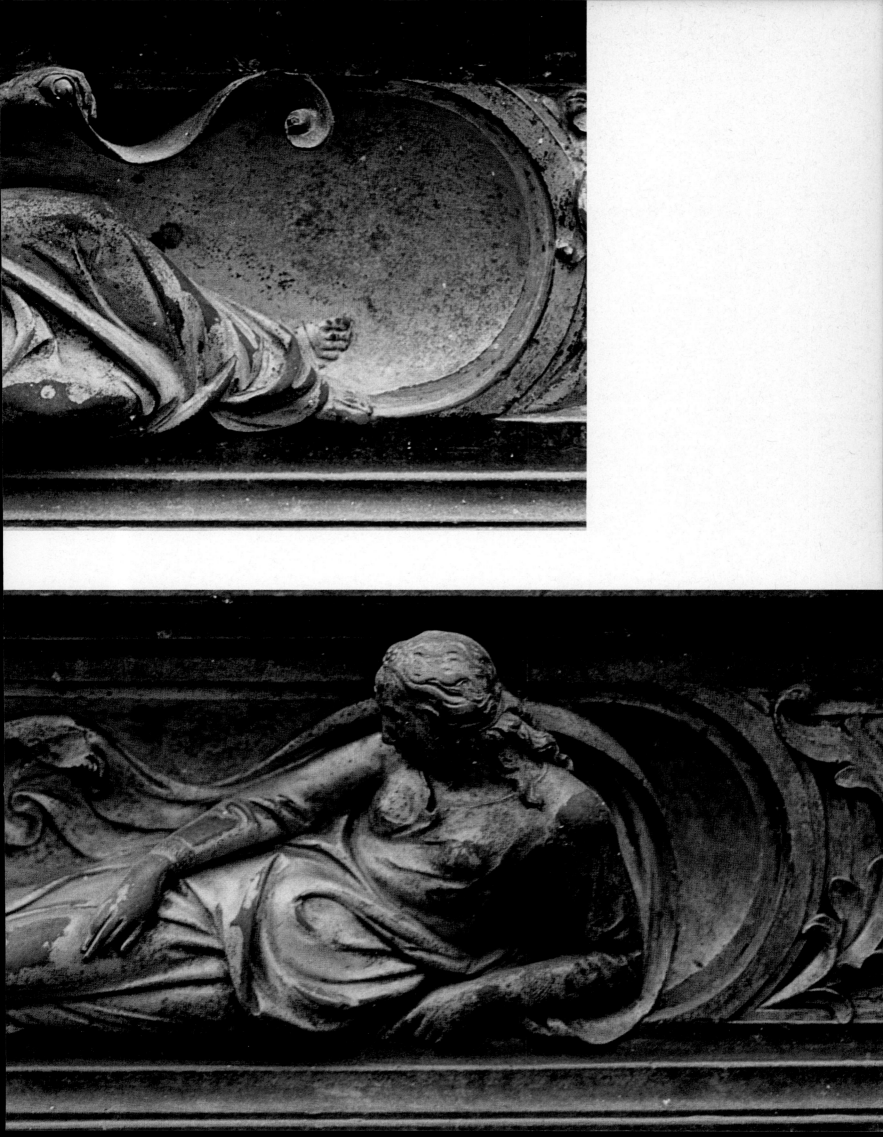

221

Genesis: Ghiberti's representation of the beginnings of history concentrates on mankind's part and role in the world from the creation of the universe, and puts divine activities quite literally in the background. From the lower left corner, where an anthropomorphized Yahweh creates Adam, through the panel's centre and God's raising up Eve out of the body of the sleeping Adam, the principal focus of action moves, as though Ghiberti were impatient to establish the *need* for the prophets and prefigurations of the rest of the Old Testament, to the expulsion of the first couple from Paradise. Adam and Eve are clearly the important personages in Ghiberti's view of the creation, more to be emphasized than the fact, or mystery, of creation itself. The creating Yahweh, floating above the scene in a mystical, neo-Platonic rainbow of concentric circles, carries a rod and wears a strange headdress that give him the look of a medieval Gnostic magician; he puts aside these accoutrements when he creates Adam and Eve. Satan, too, theriomorphic half-serpent, half-human, looks more like a storybook character than the fallen greatest of all the angels, and stands in contrast to the literally portrayed humanity of Yahweh with Adam or with Eve. Once the fatal apple had been eaten, Adam and Eve advanced a step in recognizing their humanity: they became aware of their sexuality, a change Ghiberti records in the girdle of leaves each of them wears as they leave Paradise. They have realized their nakedness; as Satan had promised Eve, their eyes were opened. Finally, through a severely stylized arch the wretched couple are driven by the most flamboyant of the panel's angels. *Details: 223 God creating Eve; 224 Adam; 225 angel; 226 Eve; 227 Adam and Eve and the serpent; 228 angels; 229 angels*

223

225

228

229

Cain and Abel: Once Adam and Eve had awakened to their sexuality, they had intercourse, and Eve bore a son. In a play on the word for 'get' or 'acquire', he was named Cain: 'With Yahweh's help I have acquired a man-child.' Later, she gave birth to her second son, Abel. Cain tilled the soil, while Abel tended the family's flocks. Of their labours they sacrificed to Yahweh, Cain some of the produce of the fields, but Abel the first-born of his flocks. In a bias that runs through the whole Bible, Yahweh preferred the younger son and his offering. Out of envy, Cain killed Abel and was banished by Yahweh.

Ghiberti interprets this story in a pair of opposing triangles: the upper, inverted, one begins above left with Adam and Eve and the child Cain outside their shelter; Abel, with his dog, sits tending his flock; and Cain and Abel sacrifice by burning offerings, while Yahweh turns his face to Abel. The lower triangle is clearly Cain's story: at the lower left he ploughs his fields with two oxen; upwards at the right, he swings a heavy club at the already fallen Abel, about to kill him; at the lower right, now using his club as a staff, he gestures in what Ghiberti seems to imply is remonstrance, at Yahweh whose right arm is extended in a sweeping, banishing gesture. Ghiberti's dialogue here between Cain and Yahweh reproduces the subtlety of argument in the Bible narrative. When Yahweh, in punishment for the slaying of Abel, banished Cain, cursing him to a life of wandering, the murderer objected that anyone who came across him would murder him. At that, Yahweh put a mark on Cain, not as a sign of shame, but as a token that 'if anyone kills Cain, sevenfold vengeance shall be taken for him'. The 'mark of Cain', then, indicates the blood-price to be exacted for the murder of Cain or any member of his tribe. Ghiberti concentrates, as in the *Genesis* panel, the climax and implied consequences of this story at the lower right. *Details: 231 Cain ploughing; 232 oxen; 233 Cain cursed; 234 Yahweh; 235 Abel; 236 Adam and Eve with Cain*

231

235

236

Noah: Nine generations after Adam, in a direct line from his son Seth who was born to replace the murdered Abel, Noah was born at a time when Yahweh saw that the heart of man 'fashioned nothing but wickedness all day long'. At Yahweh's command, Noah built an ark, put on board his family and 'of all the clean animals, seven of each kind, both male and female, and of the unclean animals, two, a male and its female', and 'Yahweh closed the door behind Noah.' For forty days and nights it rained, and the rains flooded the earth, killing everything on its face. At last, the rains stopped, the waters receded, and Noah, his family and all the animals left the ark. Ghiberti fills the upper part of his panel with this episode of the story, filling the bulk of that space with the unusual pyramidal ark, which can easily be misconstrued for rays of light pouring down onto the earth. Yahweh, at the upper right, leans down from his rainbow circle to acknowledge and accept the sacrifice of a ram which Noah and his sons and daughters, at bottom right, are about to offer. The rainbow, Yahweh told Noah after the flood, was to be a sign of his covenant with men from that time on: 'When the bow appears in the clouds, I shall recall the covenant between myself and you, and every living creature.' In his selection of events in Noah's story, Ghiberti appears to emphasize the covenant, whose history will unfold on this door, rather than the more spectacular chronicle of the flood.

Noah was the first to plant the vine, and Ghiberti shows him sleeping in drunken nakedness, leaning against a barrel beneath an arbour. When his son Ham came on him thus, he did nothing but went and told his two brothers. Taking a garment and, as Ghiberti shows them here, walking backwards so as not to see their father's shame, Shem and Japheth went and covered him. When he woke and discovered what had happened, Noah cursed Ham, the ancestor of the Canaanites, and gave his blessing to the other two, singling out Shem (whence our word 'semitic') for special favour. Shem was to be the ancestor of Abraham and of the Israelites who would enjoy Yahweh's special protection. Ghiberti thus, again, focuses on the essential aspects of Noah's story, moving forward the organic history of the Old Testament.

Details: 238 Noah's drunkenness; 239 Noah's son with garment; 240 Noah's family; 241 stag; 242 ram; 243 animals; 244 Noah; 245 body

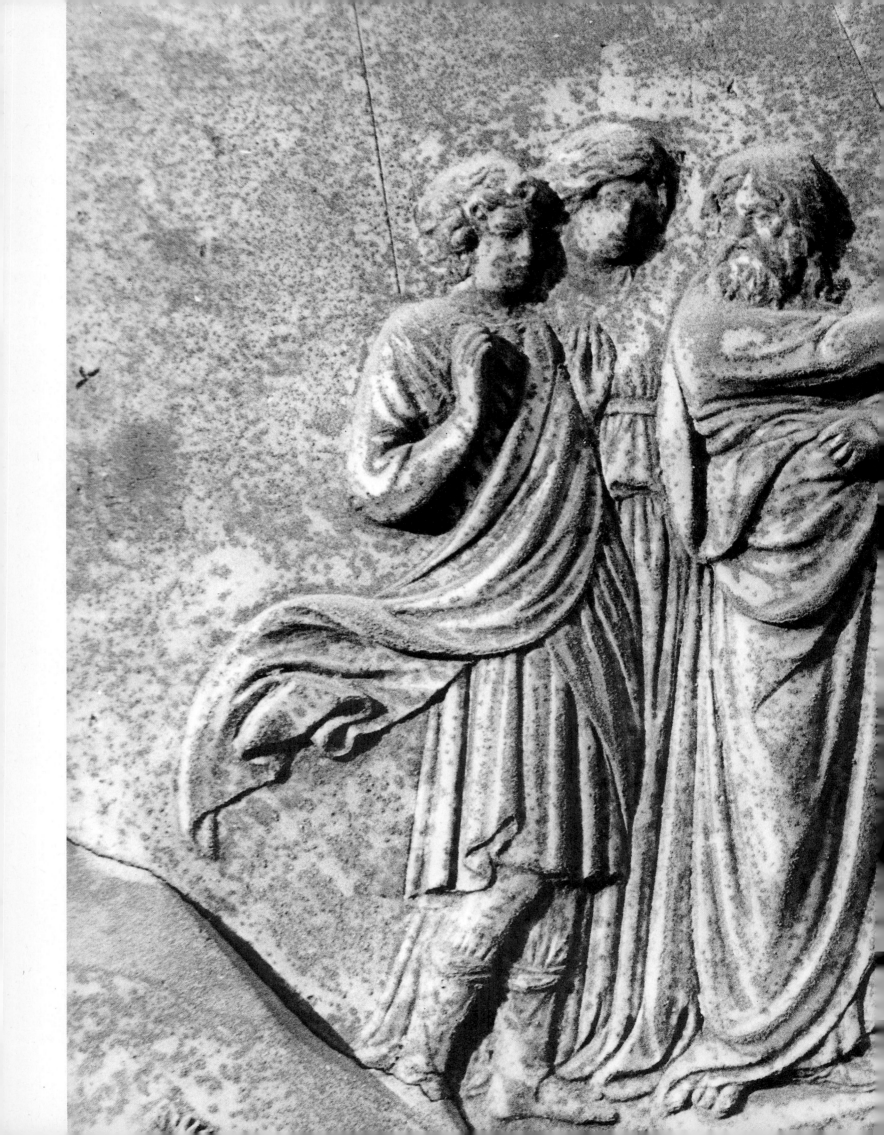

241

242

243

Abraham: After having promised him a son of his old age, whose name was to be Isaac, and confirming his covenant with mankind, Yahweh appeared to Abraham one day while he was sitting outside his tent, in the form of a man accompanied by two others. Repeating the promise of a son to Abraham, Yahweh remained with him while the other two, now angels, went to destroy Sodom and Gomorrah. Once Isaac was born, Sarah his mother became jealous of Ishmael, the son of her servant Hagar by Abraham, whom Sarah had wished to comfort for her own barrenness by urging him to conceive a child by Hagar. At Sarah's jealous instigation when she saw the two boys playing together, Abraham gave Hagar some food and water and sent her and Ishmael away. Then Yahweh appeared to Abraham and demanded the sacrifice of Isaac, who was now his only child.

As the obedient Abraham raised his hand to draw the sacrificial knife across the boy's throat, an angel appeared, told Abraham that Yahweh wished only to test his devotion, and pointed out a ram which he should sacrifice in Isaac's stead.

With consummate economy and precision, Ghiberti has reduced this long and crucial story of Abraham to the minimum of incident and detail. At the left, Sarah leaves their tent as Abraham kneels to welcome his three visitors. Ghiberti chooses to portray them as angels, perhaps because by his day they were piously considered to have been the Three Persons of the Trinity, a doctrine which was revealed only in the New Testament. Diagonally opposite this encounter, Ghiberti places the fateful obedience of Abraham, the angel's outstretched hand arresting the sacrificial knife in its downward swing. Below, in the lower right corner, are the two servants and the mule which Abraham took with him to the intended sacrifice of Isaac. There is in this group, however, particularly in the importance Ghiberti gives them and the apparently emphasized conversation between them, an overtone of the friendship between Isaac and Ishmael which so irritated Sarah. It may be that the sculptor was once again drawing attention to the motif of the rivalry between brothers, and their separation, which had figured in the previous panels' stories as it will, crucially, in the next two.

Details: 247 Isaac; 248 angels

247

249   PANEL V

Isaac: Abraham's son, Isaac, was forty years old when he married Rebecca. After twenty years of barrenness, Rebecca conceived twins, who struggled within her so that she prayed to Yahweh, who told her that there were two nations in her womb, which would be rivals, the elder serving the younger. Of the two sons Esau, the elder, was hairy and robust in nature and physique, while his brother Jacob was more comely and content to stay at home. Isaac preferred Esau, who was a hunter, while Rebecca favoured Jacob. One day, as he returned from the hunt hungry, Esau came upon Jacob eating and, in his hunger, bartered his birthright as elder son for Jacob's food. As Isaac grew older, he became blind. He called Esau to him one day, and told him to go out hunting and to prepare for him a meal of game, his favourite food, in return for which he would give Esau his blessing, as he felt he would soon die. Rebecca overheard this conversation, and once Esau had left called her favourite Jacob to her, telling him to go to the flocks and bring back two kids so that she might cook them for Isaac who would then give Jacob his blessing. Although he knew Isaac was blind and would not see him, Jacob realized that if his father once touched him he would recognize – because he was smooth-skinned – that he was not Esau.

Rebecca insisted, however, and once she had cooked the kids, she covered Jacob's arms and neck with their skins. The deception worked, and Isaac blessed Jacob, instead of Esau, who thus not only had bargained away his birthright and lost his father's blessing, but became subject to his younger brother, the favourite – like Abel and Isaac before him – of their mother.

Ghiberti moves his record of this drama from the upper right, where Rebecca on the rooftop prays to Yahweh about the conflict in her womb, to the interior of the house, and Rebecca's confinement, the bargain between Jacob and Esau at the centre, followed by Rebecca instructing Jacob about the kid he holds, while Esau, his bow on his shoulder and quiver at his waist, goes off to hunt at Isaac's request. Outside the house – in greatest detail and highest emphasis on the fraternal conflict – Ghiberti shows Rebecca witnessing Isaac's blessing of Jacob and, in the foreground at the centre, the cheated Esau with his dogs confronting the duped, and apparently apologetic, Isaac.

Details: 250 Esau confronts Isaac; 251 Rebecca; 252 Esau; 253 Esau bartering his birthright; 254 arches; 255 Rebecca praying

250

253

Joseph: Jacob married two wives, Leah and her sister Rachel. Leah bore him six sons; the slave girl of Rachel, Bilhah, bore him two, while the slave of Leah, Zilpah, likewise bore him two. Finally, 'Yahweh remembered Rachel', and she had a son, who was named Joseph, and much later another, Benjamin, in whose birth she died. Jacob loved Joseph more than all his other sons, and they at first conspired to kill him, out of jealousy. Instead, they threw him into a well, and later sold him as a slave to some Ishmaelites, who took him to Egypt where he was in turn sold into the household of Potiphar, an official of Pharaoh. Because of his cleverness, and diligence, Joseph was given complete charge over all of Potiphar's household; very soon he was made governor of all Egypt because his skill in interpreting Pharaoh's dreams had averted famine. The famine struck other countries, however, and old Jacob had twice to send his sons to Egypt to buy grain. Joseph recognized his brothers on each of their visits, though they did not know him. On the second occasion, as the brothers were leaving to return home, Joseph had his own silver cup hidden in one of the sacks of grain, the sack belonging to Benjamin, who had been born after Joseph's disappearance and so was now his aged father's favourite. When Joseph had the brothers' caravan stopped and the sacks of grain examined, the cup was,

of course, discovered, to their confusion and consternation. Hearing his brothers plead for Benjamin, and for their father who loved the boy, Joseph wept and finally revealed himself to them. He went back to Jacob's house and was united with his father.

Ghiberti makes the visual and thematic focus of Joseph's story grain: the large circular storehouse occupies most of the panel's space and draws most attention. At the upper right, Joseph is drawn from the well while one of his brothers bargains with an Ishmaelite, whose camel stands by. In the right foreground, Joseph supervises the loading of his brothers' caravan. The discovery of Joseph's cup, in the left foreground, gives Ghiberti an opportunity to reveal how well and carefully he knows the Bible story (as, indeed, his fellow Florentines would have also); in the distressed figure tearing his garments he reproduces exactly a small detail of the biblical narrative: when the cup was found, Genesis says, 'they tore their clothes'. Joseph reveals himself to his brothers at the upper left, while one of the penitent elder brothers prostrates himself to beg forgiveness.

Details: 257 officials; 258 woman with grain; 259 storehouse arches; 260 Joseph sold by his brothers; 261 brother; 262 men with grain

258

259

261

Moses: Of all the many events in the life of Moses – from his finding as an infant by Pharaoh's daughter to his death in Moab within sight of the Promised Land – Ghiberti has singled out a single incident, the Giving of the Law, for this panel representing the great Patriarch's life. Though all the other panels in the Gates of Paradise are pastiches of their subjects' lives, with the principal character appearing perhaps several times, here Ghiberti concentrates on the event which was unique to Moses: he spoke with God and brought tangible evidence of that conversation. High at the top of the panel is the summit of Mount Horeb, or Sinai, where God in a dense cloud manifested himself to Moses and gave to him the tablets of the Law for the Chosen People. Once again, as in the *Genesis* panel, God appears wearing the mitre-like headdress of omniscient authority: with the Law, the created universe is further ordered and its unity is now given a personal point of reference. The Creator-Lawgiver's accompanying angels and celestial trumpeters underline the authority and universality of the occasion: this is not a case of special intervention in the life of an individual or a family, but affects the whole of mankind. As the Israelites mill about in awed confusion at the foot of the mountain – perhaps Ghiberti wished to recall the Red Sea by the water at the lower left? – Moses stands, upright and dignified atop Horeb, between Yahweh and the Israelites, 'because they were afraid'. God had warned Moses not to let the people pass beyond their own bounds, but told him to bring up his brother Aaron, who here crouches in wonder at the 'peals of thunder and the lightning flashes, the sound of the trumpet and the smoking mountain' accompanying the theophany. The group of young women to the left, usually known as 'the Daughters of Israel', recalls the daughters of Jethro, whose sheep the young Moses had watered when they had been prevented from doing so by ruffians, and one of whom, Zipporah, Moses had later married.

Details: 264 angels; 265 woman and child; 266 woman; 267 Israelites; 268 Moses receiving the Law; 269 Aaron

269

Joshua: After Moses' death, Yahweh appointed Joshua his successor as leader of the people of Israel, whom he was divinely ordered to lead across the Jordan into the land Yahweh had promised. On the other side of the Jordan, in the land of Canaan, was the strong city of Jericho, which had first to be conquered. At Yahweh's command, Joshua had the priests carry the Ark of the Covenant to the Jordan, whose waters parted once their feet touched it. The priests remained on the now dry riverbed, at mid-Jordan, while the Israelites crossed over. As a memorial to themselves and their children of this miraculous crossing, Joshua and the people were told to have twelve men each take a stone from the bed of the river, to be set down on the opposite bank.

Once they had got to the walls of Jericho, the people, at Joshua's instructions under command of Yahweh, marched round the strong walls of the city once a day for six days; they were led by the priests carrying the Ark, who were themselves preceded by seven other priests carrying trumpets. All this was done in complete silence. On the seventh day, however, the procession walked round Jericho's walls seven times, and at the seventh time the priests sounded the trumpets and the people raised a war cry. At that moment the walls of Jericho collapsed, and Joshua and the people of Israel stormed the city in a frontal attack and captured it.

Ghiberti's Joshua stands in his chariot at mid-left, behind the Ark; at the top of the panel, he is marching in the procession of the seventh day, while the priests sound their trumpets; great cracks appear in Jericho's walls, and one of its towers is falling. At the panel's centre, the dry and stony bed of the Jordan lies waiting for some of the Israelites to cross it, while six of the twelve leaders of Israel reach the bank carrying the memorial stones. The pyramidal shape of the upper part of the Ark of the Covenant here echoes the form Ghiberti gave to Noah's ark, repeating and emphasizing the fact and importance of Yahweh's covenant with his chosen people to whom, Ghiberti reminds us in this similarity, Yahweh first showed special favour in the days of Noah.

Details: 271 women; 272 women about to cross the Jordan; 273 Israelite men; 274 leader with stone; 275 women outside tent; 276 Joshua in the procession

271

272

274

275

276

277 PANEL IX

David: David the shepherd, youngest son of Jesse, was chosen by the prophet Samuel to succeed Saul as king of the Israelites. The boy was taught and nurtured by Samuel against the day of his succession. When war broke out between the Israelites and the Philistines, Saul led his army into battle, armed and swaggering. Goliath of Gath, the Philistines' champion who was more than eight feet (2.5 metres) tall, wore a helmet of brass and scale-armour, and carried a lance as long and heavy as a weaver's beam, taunted the Israelites to send their best man against him. David volunteered to accept the challenge and, despite Saul's protests, went to confront the giant. At first, Saul had given the youth his own armour; David, however, objected that he could not even walk in it, and took it off. Instead, he picked five smooth stones from the river bed, put them in his shepherd's pouch over his shoulder, and went out to meet Goliath carrying his sling. With the first stone he drew from his pouch, David killed Goliath – the stone penetrated his forehead – and, using the giant's own sword, cut off his head. The Israelites were exultant at this victory and, as David carried Goliath's head while the armies of Saul returned in triumphal procession to their homes, the women from all the towns came out, singing and dancing to the sound of tambourines, shouting, 'Saul has killed his thousands, and David his tens of thousands.'

Ghiberti gives first emphasis to David's conquest of Goliath in this panel, choosing out of all the events of the Psalmist-King's life his decapitation of the fallen giant. Once again the artist delicately stresses the favour shown to an apparently inconsequential male, not least of all in the contrast he draws between David and the standing, swaggering Saul, in a chariot on the left, who plays little or no part in this event. All of the details of the incident Ghiberti carefully, but with perfect naturalness, reproduces: David's youth, his pouch over his shoulder and sling on the ground at his right foot, Goliath's armour and great lance. At the top of the panel, outside the walls of Jerusalem, a number of Israelite women have come out to acclaim David, who carries Goliath's enormous head; one of the women accompanies her praise by striking a tambourine.

Details: 278 soldier; 279 soldier; 280 archer; 281 horses' heads; 282 David with Goliath's head; 283 triumphal procession; 284 Jerusalem; 285 Saul; 286 Jerusalem

282

285

287 PANEL X

Solomon: When Solomon, one of David's sons and his successor as king of Israel, had finished building the Temple at Jerusalem and the royal palace, he was visited by the Queen of Sheba. Solomon, the Book of Kings says, 'loved many foreign women', and indeed the first of his seven hundred marriages was to a daughter of Pharaoh. The land of Sheba was the lower part of what is now known as the Arabian peninsula, and was that Saba, or 'the East', from which it was prophesied people would come to worship the Messiah bearing 'gold and frankincense'. The Queen's gifts to Solomon included gold and 'more spices than were ever again given to the king'.

Ghiberti places the meeting between the representatives of Yahweh's people and the Gentile East in what could be the outer porches of Solomon's palace. In many respects, the building here is very similar to the palace as described in Kings, and it includes a domestic touch in the two curious servants looking down on the foreigners' arrival from upper window. Apart from the musicians at the right, there is little activity in the panel, and even the horses, which Ghiberti may have introduced as reminders that Solomon had twelve thousand of them in his stables, are quiet, considering the great press of people surrounding them. Instead of activity, Ghiberti apparently has chosen to emphasize his two principal characters. By ending the sequence of this door as it began, with an encounter between a man and a woman, he has maintained and closed a basic thematic unity; furthermore, the joined hands of Solomon and the Queen imply a reconciliation not only of the Gentiles with Israel, but also, in a more symbolic way, of the future Messiah with all people.

Details: 288 men at extreme left; 289 women beneath canopy; 290 horse and rider; 291 soldier; 292 horseman's head; 293 men; 294 women; 295 men on upper level; 296 crowd; 297 palace; 298 soldier; 299 bearded men; 300 musicians

288

292

298

299

301

302

303

304

307

BIBLIOGRAPHY

Few of the specialized works on Ghiberti, Andrea Pisano or the Baptistery doors are in English, and many are in periodicals not readily accessible to the general reader. Fortunately, however, the fullest account of Ghiberti in any language is that by R. Krautheimer and T. Krautheimer-Hess, *Lorenzo Ghiberti* (2 volumes), published at Princeton in 1956 (revised edition 1970). This contains an exhaustive bibliography (from which that given below is largely drawn), transcripts of relevant documents and 286 illustrations. A much shorter paperback by R. Krautheimer, *Ghiberti's Bronze Doors*, Princeton 1971, presents his main findings in a popular form. L. Goldschneider's *Lorenzo Ghiberti*, London 1949, contains many large, good-quality photographs. Andrea Pisano's work is far less often reproduced than Ghiberti's. But the *McGraw-Hill Encyclopaedia of World Art*, Rome and New York 1959, includes articles on both Ghiberti (by R. Krautheimer) and Andrea Pisano, under his real name, Andrea da Pontedera (by J. Pope-Hennessy), each with copious illustrations and full bibliographies. For the background of Italian sculpture of this period, see C. Seymour, *Sculpture in Italy, 1400–1500* (Pelican History of Art, Harmondsworth and Baltimore 1966). For the Baptistery, the best account is that in W. and E. Paatz, *Die Kirchen von Florenz, ein Kunstgeschichtliches Handbuch*, Frankfurt-am-Main 1940 *ff*.

Brunetti, G. *Ghiberti*, Florence 1966

Carocci, G. 'Le porte del Battistero di Firenze e l'ornamento imitato della natura', *Arte italiano decorativa e industriale*, V (1896), pp. 69 *ff*.

Falk, I. *Studien zu Andreas Pisano*, Hamburg 1940

Falk, I. and Lanyi, J. 'The Genesis of Andrea Pisano's Bronze Doors', *Art Bulletin*, XXV (1943), pp. 132 *ff*.

Fiocco, G. 'Le porte d'oro del Ghiberti', *Rinascimento*, VII (1956), pp. 3–11

Gaye, G. 'Die Bronzteuren des Lorenzo Ghiberti' in A. Reumont's *Italien*, II (1840), p. 273

Ghiberti, Lorenzo *I Commentarii*, ed. O. Morisani, Naples 1947

Lanyi, J. 'L'ultima opera di Andrea Pisano', *L'Arte*, N.S. IV (1933), pp. 204 *ff*.

Lumachi, A. *Memorie storiche dell'antichissima Basilica di San Giovanni Battista in Firenze*, Florence 1782

Marangoni, M. 'Relievi poco noti nella seconda Porta di S. Giovanni in Firenze', *Rassegna d'arte*, XI (1911), pp. 31 *ff*.

Patch, T. and Gregori, F. *La porta principale del Battistero di S. Giovanni*, Florence 1773

Planiscig, L. *Lorenzo Ghiberti*, Vienna 1940 (Italian ed., Florence 1949)

Poggi, G. *La Porta del Paradiso di Lorenzo Ghiberti*, Florence 1949

——— 'La ripulitura delle porte del Battistero Fiorentino', *Bolletino d'arte*, XXXIII (1948), pp. 244 *ff*.

Rossi, F. 'The Baptistery Doors in Florence', *Burlington Magazine*, LXXXIX (1947), pp. 334 *ff*.

Sirén, O. 'Ghiberti's Förste Bronzeporte', *Tilskueren*, XXV (1908), pp. 834 *ff*.

Toschi, G. B. 'Le Porte del Paradiso', *Nuova Antologia di scienze, lettere ed arti*, ser. 2, XV (1879), pp. 449 *ff*.

Venturi, L. 'Lorenzo Ghiberti', *L'Arte*, XXVI (1923), pp. 233 *ff*.

Wundram, M. *Die Paradiestür*, Stuttgart 1962

DETAILS FROM THE DECORATED BORDERS

with plate numbers

Except where indicated, all numbers refer to illustration numbers; page numbers are in brackets

The illustrations to Kenneth Clark's introduction have been provided by the following:
Alinari, pp. 9, 10, 13, 15; Arch. Vat., p. 14; Bildarchiv Foto Marburg, p. 9; British Musuem, London, p. 11.